I0136528

Philadelphia Railroad

Summer excursion routes via the valley of the Schuylkill and

the Catawissa route

Philadelphia Railroad

Summer excursion routes via the valley of the Schuylkill and the Catawissa route

ISBN/EAN: 9783337145484

Printed in Europe, USA, Canada, Australia, Japan

Cover: Foto ©Andreas Hilbeck / pixelio.de

More available books at **www.hansebooks.com**

Philadelphia & Reading Railroad.

SUMMER EXCURSION ROUTES

VIA THE

Valley of the Schuylkill and the Catawissa Route,

AND VIA THE

VALLEYS OF THE SCHUYLKILL, THE PERKIOMEN, AND THE LEHIGH.

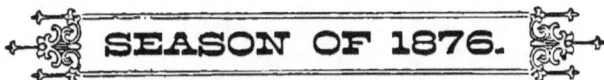

SEASON OF 1876.

Where to Go, What to See, How Much it Costs.

OVER 300 ROUTES.

COMPRISING TOURS THROUGH THE

COAL AND MOUNTAIN REGIONS OF PENNSYLVANIA,	TRENTON FALLS,
MINNEQUA SPRINGS,	AU SABLE CHASM,
WATKINS' GLEN,	RIVIERE DU LOUP,
NIAGARA FALLS,	SAGUENAY RIVER,
SENECA and CAYUGA LAKES,	THOUSAND ISLANDS,
LAKES GEORGE and CHAMPLAIN,	MONTREAL and QUEBEC,
SARATOGA and RICHFIELD SPRINGS,	WHITE MOUNTAINS,
SWITCHBACK R. R., MAUCH CHUNK,	BOSTON and PORTLAND,
GLEN ONOKO,	NEWPORT and HUDSON RIVER,
	LONG ISLAND SOUND.

Tickets on sale from June 1st to October 30th, 1876, good to return until November 30th, 1876.

PASSENGERS HAVE ALL THE PRIVILEGES OF FIRST CLASS TICKETS.

CENTENNIAL EDITION.

J. E. WOOTTEN,
General Superintendent, Reading.

C. G. HANCOCK,
General Ticket Agent, Philadelphia.

ALPHABETICALLY ARRANGED.

COAL AND MOUNTAIN REGION EXCURSIONS.

GENERAL EXCURSIONS.

EXTENSION OR SIDE-TRIP TICKETS.

Alexandria Bay (Thousand Islands), Au Sable Chasm, Cacouna, Clayton (Thousand Islands), Glen Onoko, Ha-Ha Bay, Lake George and Fort Ticonderoga, Montreal, Ottawa City, Paul Smith's, Quebec, Sackett's Harbor, St. Alban's, Stowe, Tadousac, Trenton Falls.

SEA-SHORE EXCURSIONS.

Atlantic City, Barnegat, Beach Haven, Cape May, Long Branch, New York and Long Branch, Long Branch and Newport.

DESCRIPTION OF SCENERY AND PLACES OF INTEREST

ON THE

PHILADELPHIA & READING RAILROAD AND BRANCHES.

OW little the above title serves to inform the reader of the extent of track controlled by this road, its branches and connections! It is sufficient to say here, that the distance from Philadelphia to Reading is fifty-eight miles, while the approximate aggregate of miles of track owned, leased, and operated is fifteen hundred.

The two city depots of this Company are located at Broad and Callowhill and Ninth and Green streets. From the former through trains leave and arrive via Reading, Harrisburg, Williamsport, Lancaster, Columbia, and points in New York State and the West, while the latter depot is the

THE SCHUYLKILL FROM COLUMBIA BRIDGE.

(3)

FALLS BRIDGE.

starting and arriving point of the through trains via the new and popular
Perkiomen Route to and from Allentown, Mauch Chunk, Wilkesbarre, Elmira,
all points on the Lehigh Valley Railroad, Erie Railway, points in New York
State, the West and North-west.

WISSAHICKON CREEK.

On the route from Broad and Callowhill we cross the Schuylkill at Columbia
Bridge, while on the route from Ninth and Green we cross the same river at the
Falls of Schuylkill. Between the two points is Belmont Station, at which is

the entrance to the famous Belmont Glen, justly known as one of the finest parts of Philadelphia's great Park. Thousands from the city and country visit it yearly, and the "Reading Railroad Company," as it is generally styled, runs for the accommodation of visitors what are called "Park Accommodation" trains. Just beyond the Glen lie the grounds on which are erected the buildings for the Exposition incident to the Centennial Anniversary of our nation's birth. The position of this road, its facilities, conveniences, and the territory drained, seem to insure an immense trade during the continuance of the Exhibition. Southward from this point a track has been laid to the station of this Company at the Centennial Grounds,

VALLEY FORGE.

where trains will land and take up all passengers coming to or going from the Exhibition.

The station is in close proximity to five entrances to the Exhibition, and all arrangements will be made for the proper accommodation of the public.

We are now fairly on the banks of the Schuylkill,—that river of which

SCHUYLKILL RIVER ABOVE POTTSTOWN.

the poet Moore sang and wrote, on whose banks he found that rest, though slight, for which he had sought elsewhere in vain. But while we fain would quote from the writings of him who, it might. be said, immortalized this beautiful river, yet, as we have not reached a distance of five miles from our starting point, the thought of what is yet before us compels a leave-taking of Fairmount Park and Tom Moore's cottage, and with a glance at Laurel Hill Cemetery, across the river, encompassed by the eastern part of the Park, to pass on, following the windings of the river through Falls Village, Manayunk, and Conshohocken, at all of which are located large industrial establishments, until we reach Norristown.

Our station here is named Bridgeport, and is the terminus of the Chester Valley Branch; while on the opposite or Norristown side is the terminus of the Norristown Branch, which has its depot in Philadelphia at Ninth and Green streets, and which has been almost parallel with us since leaving Falls Village. The river scenery becomes finer as we leave the thriving hamlets that extend westwardly, like a chaplet of beads, from Philadelphia, and form a part of its gigantic industries. As nature begins to assert her sway over the more distant waters of our river, the charm becomes more distinctly sylvan and bucolic. The current slips through a green garden, idle as a ribbon that lies on a beauty's lap, and all is like a dream of contentment.

We now reach Valley Forge, so memorable for the sufferings of the patriot army under Washington during the winter of 1777-8. The country throughout this section is filled with historical recollections, and many a Revolutionary story, handed down from generation to generation, can be told to a ready listener. Just above this point the Perkiomen creek empties into the river. The valley through which this creek flows is noted for its unusually beautiful scenery, and its mineral and agricultural resources. It was the abode for many years of Audubon, the great naturalist, in whose works reference is made to many of the rare birds seeking rest and shelter there.

The Perkiomen Branch follows the line of the creek named for about twenty-three miles, and abounds with picturesque views from hill and dale. Here the humble abode of the steady and industrious farmer, whose well-tilled ground gives evidence of his success; here a neat small town with ancient church, the spire of which marks the village from afar; here some creek, tributary to the Perkiomen, taking its winding way through the hills; then the hills themselves, silent and majestic, guarding the valleys and those who inhabit them.

Collegeville, a place of considerable summer resort, six miles from Perkiomen Junction, is a thriving town, containing a number of fine boarding-houses, where good accommodations can be had during the summer months.

Ursinus College, under the direction of the German Reformed Church, is located at this point.

Schwenksville, Green Lane, Pennsburg, Zionsville, and Emaus are all places of fair size,—Pennsburg and Emaus being the largest and most important.

Allentown is the terminus of this branch and point at which connection is made with the Lehigh Valley Railroad, thus forming a new line to the Valley of the Lehigh, to points in New York State, the West, North-west, and Canada. It contains a population of fifteen thousand people and is the county town of Lehigh county; is situated on the south bank of the Lehigh river at the mouth of Jordan creek. The streets are regularly and tastefully laid out, being broad and clean and well shaded. A fine public square is in the centre of the city; in addition to which the presence of gas-lamps, hydrants, and horse-cars gives it an unmistakably metropolitan air. Here, too, we find in the stone bridge eighteen hundred feet long, spanning the Jordan creek by nineteen arches, the largest structure of the kind in the State. Among its industries Allentown boasts ten rolling-mills and iron-works, as well as woolen and planing mills, carriage and sash factories, and a host of similar minor establishments. It has three national banks, a handsome court-house and jail, three costly public school-houses, eighteen churches, nearly a dozen newspapers, Odd Fellows' and Masonic halls, a fine opera-house, and numerous other showy public edifices. The fair grounds, covering twelve acres in the outskirts of the city, contain a fine exhibition building, known as Floral

SCHUYLKILL RIVER BELOW READING.

Hall, a race-track, and stalls for one hundred head of horses and cattle. Among the private educational establishments, Muhlenburg College, founded in 1848, and the Allentown Female College are prominent. The scenery and natural curiosities of the city are well worth seeing. There are several romantic springs near by, much resorted to by strangers; and from Bauer's Rock, close at hand, one may look down from an elevation of a thousand feet upon the rich and varied landscapes of the Saucon and Lehigh Valleys.

At Allentown we connect with the Lehigh Valley Railroad for Slatington, Mauch Chunk, the Switchback Railroad, Wilkesbarre, Scranton, Waverly, Elmira, and Sayre. From the latter connections are made for Oswego, Geneva, and points on the New York Central Railroad; while from Elmira connections are made with the Erie Railway for Buffalo, Rochester, Niagara Falls, points in Canada, the West and North-west. Watkins' Glen, twenty-two miles from Elmira, is reached over the Northern Central Railway. Let us now return to the main line of our road.

Phœnixville (terminus of the Pickering Valley Branch, eleven miles in length), at which is located one of the largest rolling-mills in the United States,—that of the Phœnix Iron Company,—is situated at the mouth of French creek, which flows through a remarkably fertile valley. The station here is of brown stone, and has a very attractive appearance. The .train,

MOUNT CARBON.

leaving the main track, runs directly under the sheds, thus preventing any danger from passing trains. Shortly after leaving this last-named point we pass into a tunnel, from which we emerge to cross the river to the bank opposite to that on which we have been traveling since leaving Belmont, and passing on through Pottstown, where the shops of the roadway department are located, and Douglassville, we cross, near their mouths, the Manatawny and Monocacy creeks. The river grows more brilliant mile by mile. Finally three great hills—Mount Penn, Mount Gibraltar, and Neversink—converge to make a handsome shelter for a town; and here the river, after twisting into several curves and loops, all presenting most picturesque scenery, straightens out and introduces the city of Reading.

Reading is a city with a population of about forty thousand, and stands third in the State. For variety in manufacturing interests it probably has no

TUMBLING RUN DAM, NEAR POTTSVILLE.

rival, except Philadelphia. Here we find the rolling-mill, foundry, car, and machine shops of the Company, and a depot, without doubt, the handsomest in the State. A first-class restaurant and dining-saloon is connected therewith, affording an opportunity to satisfy the cravings of hunger and thirst.

From Reading various branches start out, all trains over which arrive and depart from the one depot. From the large electrical clock in the tower, time is communicated to every clock in the interior of the depot; consequently the passengers, ticket-sellers, train-master, engineer, conductor, and baggage-

JUST ABOVE PORT CLINTON.

master are all using the same standard of time—that of Philadelphia. In a depot like this, where trains are constantly arriving and departing in all directions, the value of such an arrangement is naturally suggestive to the intelligent mind. Here also can be seen the works at which the Company manufacture gas for use in the depot and cars.

Westward runs the Lebanon Valley Branch, fifty-four miles, to Lebanon and Harrisburg, connecting at latter point with Pennsylvania Railroad for the West, with the Northern Central Railroad for the North, as also for

MAHANOY PLANE (LOOKING UP).

Baltimore and Washington on the South, and with Cumberland Valley Railroad. South of Lebanon, a distance of six miles, are the Cornwall ore deposits, comprised in three mountains, called Grassy Hill, Middle Hill, and Big Hill. The ore is quite on the surface, forming a deposit of three hundred and twenty-five feet on the higher parts, and thinning out on the edges of the hills. The mass covers a hundred acres, and though it has been worked for more than a century, seems inexhaustible, as the deeper treasure remains untouched. Most of it is merely shoveled, like garden mould, from the hilltop and sides, and carried by cars to the furnaces.

Diverging from the branch named at Sinking Spring, six miles from Reading, we have the Reading & Columbia Railroad, on the line of which is located Ephrata and Litiz Springs, two very popular summer resorts, at which will be found first-class hotel accommodations. This road has

RAVINE AND HEAVY GRADE NEAR FRACKVILLE.

termini at Columbia (forty-five miles) and Lancaster (forty-two miles). The former, like Harrisburg, is situated on the Susquehanna river. The valleys in which both of these branches are located, as well as that eastward from Reading to Allentown, on the Lehigh river, through which runs the East Pennsylvania Branch (thirty-six miles long), are of the greatest fertility, and are in the garden counties of the State, viz., Berks, Lancaster, Lebanon, and Lehigh, the aggregate value of whose agricultural products were in 1874 upwards of $78,000,000, while the manufacturing industries are estimated as having equaled $75,000,000. Exhibitions of varied interests to this value are rare indeed.

We have left the Schuylkill and have gone to the Susquehanna and Lehigh; let us now return to our old companion. Passing north from Reading, the farm land begins gradually to struggle with the mountains, the latter getting the final victory, with, of course, an advantage in favor of the picturesque.

RAVINO GAP.

Piercing the mountain, the road emerges at Port Clinton (seventy-eight miles from Philadelphia). Here the two forks—the Schuylkill and Little Schuylkill—join. The streams rise not far apart in the coal hills of the north, and, describing two great curves, meet at the point named. The station here is of brown stone and turreted roof, and has an exceedingly tasty and antique appearance. Fifteen miles to the northward the main line of this Company ends at Pottsville, before reaching which, however, we follow the twistings and windings of the river, passing Auburn, Schuylkill Haven, and Mount Carbon, from which various branches of the road penetrate the long valleys, seeking for coal. Pottsville (ninety-three miles from Philadelphia) has a population of about sixteen thousand, and is the centre round which revolves the immense trade of Schuylkill county. Passenger trains start several times daily, in almost all directions, and here, where the hotel accommodations are good, we would recommend as a headquarters for those who wish to spend several days in the coal regions.

LOWER GORDON PLANE.

The Mansion House at Mount Carbon, one mile short of Pottsville and the junction of various branches leading into the lower and middle coal fields, we can heartily recommend as a first-class establishment in every particular. Its situation at the foot of Sharp Mountain, its surroundings, and the views of the valleys and river, linger long in the memory of the visitor.

We now return to Port Clinton, from which, in a northerly direction, runs the Little Schuylkill Branch. The scenery here is especially wild

MINE HILL GAP—MINE HILL RAILROAD.

and romantic, and the tourist should be thankful that the pursuit of anthracite coal has caused railroads to be built through ravines and valleys which, under other circumstances, it would be almost impossible to penetrate. After traveling twenty miles, Tamaqua, a thriving town of five thousand inhabitants, is reached. Here we find a new and very tasty depot; twenty minutes is allowed for dinner, which is quite refreshing after a ride of four hours, which is the time it takes the through Williamsport Express to run from Philadelphia to this point.

To reach the thickest of the coal region, and to see the manner of mining and transporting coal, we now leave the direct line from Philadelphia to Williamsport and strike to the west, passing Mahanoy City, Girardville, Mahanoy Plane (where a branch to Shenandoah City leaves), Ashland, and Gordon, and thence out through Shamokin to Herndon, a water-side town on the Susquehanna, distant from Tamaqua sixty-three and one-half miles.

At Mahanoy Plane, as its name implies, is an inclined plane for raising coal cars from the valley to the top of the mountain, from which they run by continuous down grade to Mount Carbon, spoken of heretofore. This plane is two thousand four hundred and ten feet long, rising in perpendicular height three hundred and fifty-four feet; the summit is one thousand four hundred and seventy-eight feet above tide-water. At the head of the plane we are but

GERMANTOWN VALLEY—MINE HILL RAILROAD.

twelve miles from Pottsville by rail. The object of the plane is apparent when the distance is computed from that point around through the valleys.

Passing on through the towns enumerated, in and around which, at the collieries, is a population estimated at forty thousand people, we reach Gordon. This is the foot of the Gordon Planes, lower and upper. The lower has a length of four thousand seven hundred and fifty-five feet in a rise of four hundred and four, placing you one thousand two hundred and six feet above tide. The upper plane is somewhat shorter, though steeper, and places you one thousand five hundred and ninety feet above tide. From the top or head the coal cars are run down to Schuylkill Haven, a distance of nineteen miles.

In connection with the movements of the coal and general carrying trade of this Company on its main road and branches, it would be well to remark here that four hundred and ten locomotives, fourteen thousand nine hundred and seventy-five coal, three thousand eight hundred freight, and three hundred and ten passenger cars are required to remove it, and that during the fiscal year ending November, 1875, the tonnage of the road was, in coal, nearly six million tons, while that of merchandise was two million seven hundred thousand tons. The number of passengers carried amount to

six million nine hundred and thirty-eight
thousand ; and when we state that since the
Company has been in operation it has carried
over forty-eight millions of passengers
and never killed one, we say what we
feel quite able to maintain, that this
is more than can be truly said of any
railroad in this or in any other coun-

try. To the system
of signal-towers and
stone-ballasted
track, steel rails
have in many places
been added, while
the passenger trains
are equipped with
the Westinghouse
improved air brake,
and the Miller patent coupler, buffer,
and platform. The conductors and
train hands are efficient and polite,
are neatly uniformed, and thoroughly
understand their business. The latter
statement is, however rather super-
fluous, as the record heretofore noted is the best evidence that can be adduced
that they intelligently carry out the orders of their superiors.

Before leaving the coal regions we must refer to a section which is in the

LORBERRY JUNCTION.

valley to the westward of Gordon Planes. It is reached by leaving the main
line at Auburn, and, after passing through the Pine Grove and Lorberry
coal fields, we go up into what is called the Tower City and Brookside
region. Here, while the disgorging mines pile up their dust-heaps all
around you and the dull mules clamber to the lofty breakers with their
loads of coal, the eye commands a distance which is full of enchant-
ment. The direction of the valley is so straight that you are sure you can
see all the way down to the Susquehanna river at Harrisburg. Along the
vista the inequalities of the parallel mountain walls jut out one beyond the
other, forming accents of fainter and fainter blue in an interminable perspec-
tive, until everything faints in a horizon of blinding azure and silver,—it is a
painter's opportunity for toil and vision,—the practical and the ideal are most
artfully blended.

Let us now return to Tamaqua and start again northward, feeling, as one
does after a good dinner, at peace with all the world. In this frame of mind
we are in good condition to appreciate the beauties of the Catawissa Road,
which will soon lie before and around us. Seated in the last car, watching
the windings of the river as it toils around the mountains, we almost fail
to notice that a gradual ascent is being made. We pass East Mahanoy
Junction and reach Tamanend, where the through car from New York is
attached, having come through over the Central Railroad of New Jersey and
its Lehigh and Susquehanna and Nesquehoning Branches, via Easton, Allentown, and Mauch Chunk.

Leaving Tamanend, we pass Quakake, and, instead of being in the valleys,
are getting up among the mountain-tops, passing through tunnels, winding

THE SUSQUEHANNA NEAR HERNDON.

around curves, on some of which it appears as if the rear part of the train was chasing the engine and in danger of making a collision. Here may be seen an American forest preserved in all its wildness, and as we wind around, climbing still higher and higher, we notice how much smaller the objects in the valley appear. Here and there we find an old cabin, sadly dilapidated, probably used by hunters years ago, or by the engineers when making the survey of the railroad. Still onward and upward goes the train, twisting and darting, until the summit is reached. We now feel somewhat relieved, for we

VIEW ON THE SUSQUEHANNA OPPOSITE CATAWISSA.

have unconsciously been partaking of part of the labor and strain in getting up the mountain; every puff of the engine seemed to find an echo within us— an inclination to push or help in some way vaguely asserted itself, but now we rest and glance over what is before us. Some of the lower hills, completely cleared of forest, have been cultivated to the summit; others, in all their natural loneliness, are covered with pine trees, more stem and branch than leaves; between them the valleys, dark and lonesome, with here and there a cultivated spot, which would look very bare and forsaken were it not for the snug little farm-house nestled by the side of the hill for protection from the cold blasts of the north ; the blue smoke that so gracefully curls from the chimney speaks not of coal,—wood still holds sway as fuel in these valleys, and promises to do so for years to come.

In the valley, close to Girard Station, our attention is attracted to what, for this region, one would term a fine old homestead. This at one time was the residence of Stephen Girard, to whom Philadelphia is so greatly indebted for his magnificent charities. The ground on which it stands is, we believe, part of that which was placed in trust to the city at the time of his death.

Passing Mahanoy and Krebs Stations, we reach Ringtown, close to which is the first trestle over which the road crosses. This spans a narrow valley, and is nearly one hundred and fifty feet high. From this point up to Catawissa there is a succession of narrow valleys, which are spanned in a similar manner as that at Ringtown, excepting that at Mainville, which is crossed by a first-class truss bridge, lately completed.

It is here we get the first good view of Catawissa creek, as it rolls and lashes over its rocky channel. The scene is especially wild and picturesque. Looking, as you do, from a spot some hundred feet above, the creek seems but a narrow line along the mountains,—here and there it is lost to sight, as it twists around the base of the mountain, seeking a channel.

We are now approaching Mainville Water Gap, which, while possibly less grand than those of Delaware and Lehigh, yet shows an extremely enjoyable scene. The valley is highly cultivated, and is apparently completely surrounded. The creek seems to run straight into the mountain and then disappear from sight. We are completely hemmed in, and, while wondering which way we shall get out, we are in an instant around the mountain and the scene fades from view. As we cross the valley by the bridge, a fine view is obtained of the McAuley and Nescopeck Mountains in the distance.

A few miles beyond this Catawissa is reached. This good old town is situated on the North Branch of the Susquehanna, at the mouth of Catawissa creek. It can be best described by the quotation of a part of an article published in a magazine last year :—

"From the hill behind the old burg Thomas Moran once sketched and painted an enchanting scene—the creek in sight for fifteen miles, winding to meet the river through ravines embroidered with the dyes of an American autumn. The junction of the river and stream is here a superb scenic nucleus. Nature, after running the thread of a more narrow and continuous landscape drama, here suspends the plot, and lets fall a superb drop-curtain, painted with splendor and romance, which detains the spectator for a long while in delight and with no wish to proceed. The bluff, below the town, two hundred feet high, commands the groves of Catawissa Island, the long diorama of the river, the old stone-abutted county bridge, the railway bridge, and the banks shaded with verdure."

Crossing the Susquehanna, Rupert, a junction station, is reached. Here connection is made with trains westward to Northumberland and north-eastward to Wilkesbarre and Scranton, and by stage to Bloomsburg, a large manufacturing town, three miles distant. From here the North Branch of the Susquehanna is followed to Danville, an iron-manufacturing town, having a population of ten thousand. The value of the industrial products of Montour county for 1874 is estimated to equal upwards of $7,000,000, most, if not all, of which was produced at Danville.

We are now fairly down into the valley, and moving north-westerly through Montour and Northumberland counties,—both good agricultural districts,—we reach the West Branch of the Susquehanna, on which, at this point, is situated the town of Milton, a most attractive place to those who desire a few weeks' rest and quiet. The hotels are fair in size and very well kept, the charges being moderate.

The towns of New Columbia, Dewart, and Watsontown are now passed in rapid succession, in and around which we notice numerous saw-mills: these of course, indicate a lumber country, and as we have been gradually leaving coal and its regions, so also have we been, without apparent knowledge of it, surely creeping into the very heart of the largest lumber region in the State.

Muncy, a fast-growing water-side town, the outlet of the lumber brought by rail and water from the Muncy creek region, is well favored with direct evidence of its industries. The same may be said of Montoursville, after passing which we are in a few minutes fairly within the limits of the city of Williamsport, where this road has its northern terminus, and where it connects with the Philadelphia & Erie Railway for Lock Haven, the oil regions, Erie, and the West, and with the Northern Central Railway for Elmira, Watkins' Glen, and Canandaigua, connecting at the former with the Erie Railway, and at the latter with the New York Central Railway, for Buffalo, Rochester, Niagara Falls, and all principal points in New York State, the Dominion of Canada, and in the Western and North-western States.

Williamsport has a population of upwards of sixteen thousand. It is beautifully located on the West Branch of the Susquehanna, has a number of large hotels and fine private residences, excelling in these particulars any city of its size in Pennsylvania. The lumber business is the leading feature. A walk through what is called the "basin," among the mills, will cause you to wonder at the immensity of that interest. The stock of lumber, lath, and pickets on hand in this region, January 1st, 1874, amounted to three hundred and sixty-three million nine hundred and forty-seven thousand one hundred and sixty-five feet, of which two hundred and seventy-one million four hundred and fifty-nine thousand three hundred and fourteen feet was pine lumber. This is independent, we believe, of the quantity in the mills, which is constantly being made into flooring-boards, doors, sash, window-frames, and other classes of mill work.

This great corporation, over whose track we have passed, has many other interests than those following this article. It owns or controls one hundred and fifty-three miles of canal, and has an immense coal-shipping depot in the northern or Richmond district of Philadelphia. It owns fourteen steam-colliers, having an aggregate carrying capacity of fifteen thousand five hundred tons, in which it transports, together with canal barges, large quantities of coal to the eastern markets. It has its own shipyard for building and repairing the colliers, and within itself manufactures nearly all of the principal material used in the operation of a railroad.

EXCURSIONS TO THE COAL AND MOUNTAIN REGIONS OF PENNSYLVANIA.

ARRANGED ALPHABETICALLY.

ASHLAND.

Form F—1.—Philad'a & Reading R. R. to Ashland; returning same route.
Rate, $4.80.

CATASAUQUA.

Form 67—X.—Philad'a & Reading R. R. to Allentown; Lehigh Valley R. R. to Catasauqua; returning same route. *Rate,* $2.90.

MOUTH OF COAL-MINE.

CATAWISSA.

Form C—1.—Philad'a & Reading R. R. to Catawissa; returning same route.
Rate, $5.80.

DANVILLE.

Form D—1.—Philad'a & Reading R. R. to Danville; returning same route.
Rate, $6.20.

(26)

EASTON.

Form 66—X.—Philad'a & Reading R. R. to Allentown; Lehigh Valley R. R. to Easton; returning same route.   *Rate*, $3.00.

ELMIRA.

Form B—1.—Philad'a & Reading R. R., via "Catawissa," to Williamsport; Northern Cent. R. W. to Elmira; returning same route.   *Rate*, $10.70.

Form B—2.—Philad'a & Reading R. R. to Allentown; Leh. Val. R. R. to Waverly; Erie R. W. to Elmira; returning same route.   *Rate*, $10.70.

BOYS PICKING OUT SLATE AT THE SCREEN.

HAZLETON.

Form L.—Philad'a & Reading R. R. to Allentown; Leh. Val. R. R. to Mauch Chunk; Switchback R. R., Mauch Chunk to Mauch Chunk (round trip over Switchback R. R.); Leh. Val. R. R. to Hazleton; Leh. Val. R. R. to Quakake; Philad'a & Reading R. R. to destination (either via Port Clinton or Pottsville).

| Philadelphia, | $5.80 | Lancaster, | $5.85 |
| Harrisburg, | 6.35 | | |

Form 86—X.—Philad'a & Reading R. R. to Allentown; Lehigh Valley R. R. to Hazleton; returning same route.   *Rate*, $5.40.

HERNDON.

Form G.—Philad'a & Reading R. R. to Herndon (Trevorton Junction); Northern Cent. R. W. to Harrisburg; Penna. R. R. to Philadelphia.
Rate, $6.90.

HOKENDAUQUA.

Form 374—X.—Philad'a & Reading R. R. to Allentown; Lehigh Valley R. R. to Hokendauqua; returning same route. *Rate*, $2.95.

JEANSVILLE.

Form 378—X.—Philad'a & Reading R. R. to Allentown; Lehigh Valley R. R. to Jeansville; returning same route. *Rate*, $5.55.

KINGSTON.

Form H.—Philad'a & Reading R. R. to Allentown; Leh. Val. R. R. to Wilkesbarre (transfer to Kingston not included in ticket); Lac. & Blooms. R. R., Kingston to Northumberland; Penna. R. R. to Sunbury; Northern Cent. R. W. to Harrisburg; Penna. R. R. to Philadelphia. *Rate*, $8.30.

Form P.—Philad'a & Reading R. R. to Allentown; Leh. Val. R. R. to Wilkesbarre (transfer to Kingston not included in ticket); Lac. & Blooms. R. R., Kingston to Northumberland; Penna. R. R. to Sunbury; Northern Cent. R. W. to Harrisburg; Philad'a & Reading R. R. to Philadelphia. *Rate*, $8.30.

LAURY'S.

Form 392—X.—Philad'a & Reading R. R. to Allentown; Lehigh Valley R. R. to Laury's; returning same route. *Rate*, $3.20.

LEHIGHTON.

Form 203—X.—Philad'a & Reading R. R. to Allentown; Lehigh Valley R. R. to Lehighton; returning same route. *Rate*, $4.00.

MAHANOY CITY.

Form G—1.—Philad'a & Reading R. R. to Mahanoy City; returning same route. *Rate*, $4.35.

MAUCH CHUNK.

Form Q.—Philad'a & Reading R. R. to Allentown; Leh. Val. R. R. to Mauch Chunk (round trip over Switchback R. R.); Leh. & Sus. R. R. to Allentown; Allentown Street-Car Line to East Penna. R. R. Junction; Philad'a & Reading R. R. to destination.

Philadelphia,	$4.50	Lancaster,	$5.25
Harrisburg,	5.75		

Form R.—Philad'a & Reading R. R. to Allentown; Allentown Street-Car Line to Leh. & Sus. R. R. Depot; Leh. & Sus. R. R. to Mauch Chunk (round trip over Switchback R. R.); Leh. Val. R. R. to Allentown; Phila. & Reading R. R. to destination.

Philadelphia,	$4.50	Lancaster,	$5.25
Harrisburg,	5.75		

Form T.—Philad'a & Reading R. R. to Quakake; Leh. Val. R. R. to Mauch Chunk (round trip over Switchback R. R.); Lehigh Val. R. R. to Allentown; Philad'a & Reading R. R. to destination.

Philadelphia,	$5.35	Lancaster,	$5.40
Harrisburg,	5.90		

MAUCH CHUNK.—Continued.

Form V.—Philad'a & Reading R. R. to Tamaqua; Leh. & Sus. R. R. to Mauch Chunk (round trip over Switchback); Leh. & Sus. R. R. to Allentown; Philad'a & Reading R. R. to destination.

Philadelphia, . . . $4.95 | Harrisburg, . . . $5.50
Lancaster, ... $5.00

Form W.—Same as Form V to Mauch Chunk and over Switchback; Leh. Val. R. R. to Allentown; Philad'a & Reading R. R. to destination.

Philadelphia, ... $4.95
Harrisburg, ... 5.50
Lancaster, ... 5.00

Form X.—Same as Form V to Mauch Chunk and over Switchback; thence Leh. Val. R. R. to Allentown, and Philad'a & Reading R. R. to Philadelphia. *Rate,* $4.50.

Form Z.—Philad'a & Reading R. R. to Tamaqua; Cent. R.R. of N. J. (L. & S. Div.) to Mauch Chunk (round trip over Switchback R. R.); Leh. Val. R. R. to Easton; Penna. R. R. to Manunka Chunk; Del., Lac. & West. R. R. to Water Gap; returning same route to Phillipsburg; thence via Penna. R. R. to Philadelphia. *Rate,* $7.40.

COAL CHUTE, DUMPER, AND BREAKER.

Form Z—1.—Philad'a & Reading R. R. to Tamanend; Cent. R. R. (L. & S. Div.) to Mauch Chunk; round trip over Switchback R. R.; returning same route.

Catawissa, ... $3.20 | Watsontown, ... $4.35
Danville, ... 3.55 | Muncy, ... 4.85
Milton, ... 4.20 | Williamsport, ... 5.35

Form Z—2.—Philad'a & Reading R. R. to Allentown; Leh. Val. R. R. to Mauch Chunk; Cent. R. R. of N. J. (L. & S. Div.) to Tamaqua; Philad'a & Reading R. R. to Herndon; Northern Cent. R. W. to Harrisburg; Penna. R. R. to Philadelphia. *Rate,* $7.00.

Form Z—3.—Philad'a & Reading R. R. to Harrisburg; Northern Cent. R.W. to Herndon; Philad'a & Reading R. R. to Tamaqua; Cent. R. R. of N. J. (L. & S. Div.) to Mauch Chunk; Leh. Val. R. R. to Allentown; Philad'a & Reading R. R. to Philadelphia. *Rate,* $6.65.

MAUCH CHUNK.—Continued.

Form Z—4.—Philad'a & Reading R. R. to Tamaqua; Cent. R. R. of N. J. (L. & S. Div.) to Mauch Chunk; round trip over Switchback R. R.; returning same route. *Rate*, $4.50.

Form 69—X.—Philad'a & Reading R. R. to Allentown; Lehigh Valley R. R. to Mauch Chunk; returning same route. *Rate*, $4.20.

MINNEQUA SPRINGS.

Form 1.—Philad'a & Reading R. R., via "Catawissa," to Williamsport; Northern Cent. R. W. to Minnequa and return to Williamsport; Penna. R. R. to Sunbury; Northern Cent. R. W. to Harrisburg; Philad'a & Reading R. R. to Philadelphia. *Rate*, $11.00.

Form 1—A.—Philad'a & Reading R. R., via "Catawissa," to Williamsport; Northern Cent. R. W. to Minnequa; returning same route. *Rate*, $10.00.

Form 2.—Philad'a & Reading R. R., via "Catawissa," to Williamsport; Northern Cent. R. W. to Minnequa; returning—Northern Cent. R. W. to Williamsport; Penna. R. R. to Sunbury; Northern Cent. R. W. to Harrisburg; Penna. R. R. to Philadelphia. *Rate*, $11.00.

MT. CARMEL.

Form K—1.—Philad'a & Reading R. R. to Mt. Carmel; returning same route. *Rate*, $5.15.

COAL-BREAKER.

PENN HAVEN.

Form 376—X.—Philad'a & Reading R. R. to Allentown; Lehigh Valley R. R. to Penn Haven; returning same route.　　　　*Rate*, $4.55.

PITTSTON.

Form 80—X.—Philad'a & Reading R. R. to Allentown; Lehigh Valley R. R. to Pittston; returning same route.　　　　*Rate*, $7.00.

RINGTOWN.

Form R—1.—Philad'a & Reading R. R. to Ringtown; returning same route.　　　　*Rate*, $4.95.

SCRANTON.

Form E.—Philad'a & Reading R. R. to Harrisburg; Northern Cent. R. W. to Sunbury; Penna. R. R. to Northumberland; Lac. & Blooms. R. R. to Scranton; Leh. & Sus. R. R. to Allentown; Allentown Street-Car Line to E. Penna. R. R. Junction; Philad'a & Reading R. R. to Philadelphia.　　　　*Rate*, $9.30.

Form K.—Philad'a & Reading R. R. to Allentown; Allentown Street-Car Line to Leh. & Sus. R. R. Depot; Leh. & Sus. R. R. to Scranton; Lac. & Blooms. R. R. to Northumberland; Penna. R. R. to Sunbury; Northern Cent. R. W. to Harrisburg; Penna. R. R. to Philadelphia.　　　　*Rate*, $9.30.

Form M.—Philad'a & Reading R. R. to Rupert; Lac. & Blooms. R. R. to Scranton; Lac. & Blooms. R. R. to Lackawanna & Bloomsburg Junction; Leh. Val. R. R. to Mauch Chunk; Switchback R. R.; Mauch Chunk to Mauch Chunk (round trip over Switchback R. R.); Leh. Val. R. R. to E. Penna. R. R. Junction; Philad'a & Reading R. R. to destination.

Philadelphia,	$8.25	Lancaster,	$8.35
Harrisburg,	8.85		

Form O.—Philad'a & Reading R. R. to Allentown; Allentown Street-Car Line to Leh. & Sus. R. R. Depot; Leh. & Sus. R. R. to Scranton: Lac. & Blooms. R. R. to Northumberland; Penna. R. R. to Sunbury; Northern Cent. R. W. to Harrisburg; Philadelphia & Reading R. R. to Philadelphia.　　　　*Rate*, $9.30.

Form 88—X.—Philad'a & Reading R. R. to Allentown; Lehigh Valley R. R. to Lackawanna & Bloomsburg Junction; Del., Lac. & West. R. R. to Scranton; returning same route.　　　　*Rate*, $7.00.

SHAMOKIN.

Form J.—Philad'a & Reading R. R. to Shamokin; Sham. Val. Branch N. C. R. W. to Sunbury; Northern Cent. R. W. to Harrisburg; Penna. R. R. to Philadelphia.　　　　*Rate*, $7.25.

SHENANDOAH CITY.

Form H—1.—Philad'a & Reading R. R. to Shenandoah City; returning same route.　　　　*Rate*, $4.80.

SLATINGTON.

Form 68—X.—Philad'a & Reading R. R. to Allentown; Lehigh Valley R. R. to Slatington; returning same route.　　　　*Rate*, $3.55.

SUNBURY.

Form C.—Philad'a & Reading R. R. to Harrisburg; Northern Cent. R. W. to Sunbury; Northern Cent. R. W. (Shamokin Div.) to Shamokin; Philad'a & Reading R. R. to Philadelphia (good either via Tamaqua and Port Clinton or Tamaqua and Pottsville). *Rate*, $6.85.

SWITCHBACK.

Form Z—5.—Philad'a & Reading R. R. to Allentown; Lehigh Valley R. R. to Mauch Chunk; round trip over Switchback R. R.; returning same route. *Rate*, $4.50.

TAMANEND.

Form J—1.—Philad'a & Reading R. R. to Tamanend; returning same route. *Rate*, $4.25.

TAMAQUA.

Form E—1.—Philad'a & Reading R. R. to Tamaqua; returning same route. *Rate*, $3.95.

TREVORTON JUNCTION.

Form A.—Philad'a & Reading R. R., Philadelphia to Harrisburg; Northern Cent. R. W., Harrisburg to Trevorton Junction (Herndon); Philad'a & Reading R. R., Herndon to Philadelphia (good either via Tamaqua and Port Clinton or Tamaqua and Pottsville). *Rate*, $6.50.

WATER GAP.

Form N.—Philad'a & Reading R. R. to Rupert; Lac. & Blooms. R. R. to Scranton; Del., Lac. & West. R. R., via Water Gap (with privilege of stopping off), to Manunka Chunk; Penna. R. R. to Phillipsburg; Leh. Val. R. R., Easton to Allentown; Philad'a & Reading R. R to destination.

Philadelphia,	$7.55	Lancaster,	$7.50
Harrisburg,	8.00		

WHITE HAVEN.

Form 390—X.—Philad'a & Reading R. R. to Allentown; Lehigh Valley R. R. to White Haven; returning same route. *Rate*, $5.40.

WILKESBARRE.

Form F.—Philad'a & Reading R. R. to Harrisburg; Northern Cent. R. W. to Sunbury; Penna. R. R. to Williamsport; Philad'a & Reading R. R. to Rupert; Lac. & Blooms. R. R. to Kingston (transfer to Wilkesbarre not included in ticket); Leh. Val. R. R., Wilkesbarre to Bethlehem; N. Penna. R. R. to Philadelphia. *Rate*, $9.30.

Form 70—X.—Philad'a & Reading R. R. to Allentown; Lehigh Valley R. R. to Wilkesbarre; returning same route. *Rate*, $6.90.

WILLIAMSPORT.

Form B.—Philad'a & Reading R. R., via "Catawissa," to Williamsport; returning via same route to Philadelphia. *Rate*, $8.00.

Form D.—Philad'a & Reading R. R. to Williamsport and return to Tamanend; Leh. & Sus. R. R. to Mauch Chunk; Switchback R. R., Mauch Chunk to Mauch Chunk (round trip over Switchback R. R.); Leh. Val. R. R. to Allentown; Philad'a & Reading R. R. to Philadelphia. *Rate*, $8.85.

Form 3.—Philad'a & Reading R. R., via "Catawissa," to Williamsport; returning—Penna. R. R. to Sunbury; Northern Cent. R. W. to Harrisburg; Philad'a & Reading R. R. to Philadelphia. *Rate*, $9.00.

Form 4.—Philad'a & Reading R. R., via "Catawissa," to Williamsport; returning—Penna. R. R. to Sunbury; Northern Cent. R. W. to Harrisburg; Penna. R. R. to Philadelphia. *Rate*, $9.00.

Form 59.—Philad'a & Reading R. R. to Allentown; Leh. Val. R. R. to Mauch Chunk; Cent. R. R. of N. J. (L. & S. Div.) to Tamanend; Philad'a & Reading R. R. to Williamsport and return to Philadelphia. *Rate*, $9.00.

Form 60.—Philad'a & Reading R. R., via "Catawissa," to Williamsport and return to Tamanend; Cent. R. R. of N. J. (L. & S. Div.) to Mauch Chunk; Leh. Val. R. R. to Allentown; Philad'a & Reading R. R. to Philadelphia. *Rate*, $9.00.

First-Class Hotels

ARE

LOCATED THROUGHOUT THE SECTIONS COMPRISED IN THE FOREGOING TOURS,

AFFORDING EVERY REQUISITE

FOR

COMFORT AT MODERATE RATES.

THE

COAL AND MOUNTAIN REGION EXCURSIONS

HERETOFORE MENTIONED

Comprise Tours Through the Most Instructive, Valuable, and Picturesque Portions

OF THE

STATE OF PENNSYLVANIA.

The holders of Excursion Tickets can stop off at any point on notification to the Conductor on the Train.

LOW RATES

AND

THOROUGHLY FIRST-CLASS CONVENIENCES

Add to the Attractions of the Route.

GENERAL EXCURSIONS.

THE TOURS MENTIONED HEREAFTER

ARE

UNEXCELLED FOR VARIETY,

AND COMPRISE

The Famous Lake and Spring Regions

OF

NEW YORK STATE,

NIAGARA AND TRENTON FALLS,

THE BEST CANADIAN SCENERY,

THE THOUSAND ISLANDS,

THE GRAND SCENERY

OF

MAINE, NEW HAMPSHIRE, AND VERMONT.

(34)

PASSENGERS
GOING BEYOND NIAGARA FALLS

Leave that point at **10 A. M.** daily, except Sunday,

FOR LEWISTON,

Where connection is made with Steamer "**City of Toronto**," reaching
Toronto at 2 P. M.,

CONNECTING WITH •

RICHELIEU & ONTARIO NAVIGATION COMPANY STEAMERS,

PASSING

THE THOUSAND ISLANDS AND RAPIDS OF ST. LAWRENCE

BY DAYLIGHT.

The coupons between Niagara Falls and Toronto, Toronto and Kingston,
Kingston and Prescott, Prescott and Montreal, and Montreal and Quebec, are
valid either by boat or rail, and they are likewise good either by the South
Shore Express Line of Steamers from Charlotte, or by the Richelieu & Ontario
Navigation Co.'s Line from Toronto.

The Tickets include Meals on Lake Ontario and the River St. Lawrence
from Toronto to Montreal, but between Montreal and Quebec they are for
passage only.

The Tickets via Plattsburgh permit the holders to remain over, thus affording tourists an opportunity to visit the Au Sable Chasm, distant 15 miles.
(See Form No. 96.)

The coupons, Profile House to Concord, going south, are good either via
stage to Littleton and thence by rail, or via stage to Plymouth and thence
by rail.

Agents are requested to specially inform passengers that the Grand Trunk
Railway and Richelieu & Ontario Navigation Co.'s Line of Steamers offer better
inducements to the traveling public than ever before. The Grand Trunk
Railway has been relaid with steel rails, and has been equipped with new
locomotives and first-class cars, and Pullman Palace Cars are run on all
Express Trains.

· A Pullman Palace Sleeping Car will be attached to the Evening Train from
Toronto, and will run through to Kingston Wharf, thus enabling passengers
to remain in the car until the boat arrives.

AMERICAN MONEY

Is taken at par at the principal hotels in Toronto, Montreal, Quebec, and
Cacouna.

GENERAL EXCURSIONS TO THE PRINCIPAL POINTS OF INTEREST IN PENNSYLVANIA, NEW YORK, THE NEW ENGLAND STATES, AND CANADA.

ARRANGED ALPHABETICALLY.

ALBANY, N. Y., AND RETURN.

Form 19 (Via Sharon Springs).—Philad'a & Reading R. R., via "Catawissa," to Williamsport; Northern Cent. R. W. to Elmira; Erie R. W. to Binghamton; Delaware & Hudson Canal and R. R. to Albany; returning—Hudson River Day or Night Boats to New York (transfer through New York not included in ticket); Penna. R. R. to Philadelphia. *Rate*, $15.10.

Form 24 (Via Seneca Lake).—Philad'a & Reading R. R. to Williamsport; Northern Cent. R. W. to Watkins'; Seneca Lake Nav. Co. to Geneva; N. Y. Cent. & Hudson River R. R. to Albany; returning—Hudson River Day Boats to New York (transfer through New York not included in ticket); Penna. R. R. to Philadelphia. *Rate*, $16.00.

Form 25 (Via Seneca Lake, returning via New York and Long Branch).—Philad'a & Reading R. R. to Williamsport; Northern Cent. R. W. to Watkins'; Seneca Lake Nav. Co. to Geneva; N. Y. Cent. & Hudson River R. R. to Albany; returning—Hudson River Day Boats to New York (transfer through New York not included in ticket); New Jersey Southern R. R. to Pemberton Junction (via Long Branch); Penna. R. R. to Philadelphia. *Rate*, $15.75.

Form 65 (Via Sharon Springs).—Philad'a & Reading R. R. to Allentown; Lehigh Valley R. R. to Waverly; Erie Railway to Binghamton; Delaware & Hudson Canal and R. R. to Albany; returning—Hudson River Day Boats to New York (transfer through New York not included in ticket); Penna. R. R. to Philadelphia. *Rate*, $13.65.

Form 66 (Via Seneca Lake).—Philad'a & Reading R. R. to Allentown; Lehigh Valley R. R. to Waverly; Erie Railway to Elmira; Northern Cent. R. W. to Watkins'; Seneca Lake Nav. Co. to Geneva; New York Cent. & Hudson River R. R. to Albany; returning—Hudson River Day Boats to New York (transfer through New York not included in ticket); Penna. R. R. to Philadelphia. *Rate*, $15.75.

Form 67 (Via Seneca Lake, returning via New York and Long Branch).—Philad'a & Reading R. R. to Allentown; Lehigh Valley R. R. to Waverly; Erie R. W. to Elmira; Northern Cent. R. W. to Watkins'; Seneca Lake Nav. Co. to Geneva; New York Cent. & Hudson River R. R. to Albany; returning—Hudson River Day Boats to New York (transfer through New York not included in ticket); New Jersey Southern R. R. to Pemberton Junction; Penna. R. R. to Philadelphia. *Rate*, $15.50.

COOPERSTOWN, N. Y.

Form 28.—Philad'a & Reading R. R. to Williamsport; Northern Cent. R. W. to Elmira; Erie R. W. to Binghamton; Delaware & Hudson Canal and R. R. to Junction; Cooperstown & Sus. Val. R. R. to Cooperstown; returning by same route. *Rate*, $13.35.

Form 70.—Philad'a & Reading R. R. to Allentown; Leh. Val. R. R. to Waverly; Erie R. W. to Binghamton; Delaware & Hudson Canal and R. R. to Junction; Cooperstown & Sus. Val. R. R. to Cooperstown; returning—Cooperstown & Sus. Val. R. R. to Junction; Delaware & Hudson Canal and R. R. to Binghamton; Erie R. W. to Elmira; Northern Cent. R. W. to Williamsport; Philad'a & Reading R. R. to Philadelphia. *Rate*, $17.40.

GENEVA, N. Y.

Form 9.—Philad'a & Reading R. R., via "Catawissa," to Williamsport; Northern Cent. R. W. to Watkins'; Seneca Lake Nav. Co. to Geneva; returning—N. Y. Cent. & Hudson River R. R. to Canandaigua; Northern Cent. R. W. to Williamsport; Penna. R. R. to Sunbury; Northern Cent. R. W. to Harrisburg; Penna. R. R. to Philadelphia. *Rate*, $15.70.

Form 10.—Philad'a & Reading R. R. to Harrisburg; Northern Cent. R. W. to Sunbury; Penna. R. R. to Williamsport; Northern Cent. R. W. to Watkins'; Seneca Lake Nav. Co. to Geneva; returning—N. Y. Cent. & Hudson River R. R. to Canandaigua; Northern Cent. R. W. to Williamsport; Philad'a & Reading R. R. to Philadelphia. *Rate*, $15.70.

Form 39 (Via Seneca Lake).—Philad'a & Reading R. R. to Williamsport; Northern Cent. R. W. to Watkins'; Seneca Lake Nav. Co. to Geneva; returning—N. Y. Cent. & Hudson River R. R. to Canandaigua: Northern Cent. R. W. to Williamsport; Philad'a & Reading R. R. to Philadelphia. *Rate*, $14.20.

Form 56.—Philad'a & Reading R. R. to Allentown; Leh. Val. R. R. to Waverly; Erie R. W. to Elmira; Northern Cent. R. W. to Watkins'; Seneca Lake Nav. Co. to Geneva; returning—N. Y. Cent. & Hudson River R. R. to Canandaigua; Northern Cent. R. W. to Williamsport; Philad'a & Reading R. R. to Philadelphia. *Rate*, $15.40.

Form 57.—Philad'a & Reading R. R., via "Catawissa," to Williamsport; Northern Cent. R. W. to Watkins'; Seneca Lake Nav. Co. to Geneva; returning—N. Y. Cent. & Hudson River R. R. to Canandaigua; Northern Cent. R. W. to Elmira; Erie R. W. to Waverly; Leh. Val. R. R. to Allentown; Philad'a & Reading R. R. to Philadelphia. *Rate*, $15.40.

MONTREAL, CANADA.

Form 32 (Via Thousand Islands; returning via Lake Champlain, Saratoga Springs).—Philad'a & Reading R. R. to Williamsport; Northern Cent. R. W. to Canandaigua; N. Y. Cent. & Hudson River R. R. to Syracuse; Rome, Watertown & Ogdenburg R. R. to Cape Vincent; Steamer "T. S. Faxton" to Alexandria Bay; Royal Mail Line to Montreal; returning—Grand Trunk R. W. to Rouse's Point; Delaware & Hudson Canal and R. R. to Plattsburg; Champlain Trans. Co. to Fort Ticonderoga; Delaware & Hudson Canal and R. R. to Albany (via Saratoga Springs); Hudson River Day Boats to New York (transfer through New York not included in ticket); Penna. R. R. to Philadelphia. *Rate*, $32.60.

MONTREAL, CANADA.—Continued.

Form 33 (Via Seneca Lake and Thousand Islands; returning via Lake Champlain, Saratoga Springs).—Philad'a & Reading R. R. to Williamsport; Northern Cent. R. W. to Watkins'; Seneca Lake Navigation Co. to Geneva; N. Y. Cent. & Hudson River R. R. to Syracuse; Rome, Watertown & Ogdensburg R. R. to Cape Vincent; Steamer "T. S. Faxton" to Alexandria Bay; Royal Mail Line to Montreal; returning—Grand Trunk R. W. to Rouse's Point; Delaware & Hudson Canal and R. R. to Plattsburg; Champlain Transportation Co. to Fort Ticonderoga; Delaware & Hudson Canal and R. R. to Albany (via Saratoga Springs); Hudson River Day Boats to New York (transfer through New York not included in ticket); Penna. R. R. to Philadelphia. *Rate,* $32.00.

Form 34 (Via Thousand Islands, Lakes George and Champlain, Saratoga Springs).—Philad'a & Reading R. R. to Williamsport; Northern Cent. R. W. to Canandaigua; N. Y. Cent. & Hudson River R. R. to Syracuse; Rome, Watertown & Ogdensburg R. R. to Cape Vincent; Steamer "T. S. Faxton" to Alexandria Bay; Royal Mail Line to Montreal; returning—Grand Trunk R. W. to Rouse's Point; Delaware & Hudson Canal and R. R. to Plattsburg; Champlain Transportation Co. to Fort Ticonderoga; Delaware & Hudson Canal and R. R. to Baldwin; Steamer "Minnehaha" to Caldwell; Stage to Glens Falls; Delaware & Hudson Canal and R. R. to Albany (via Saratoga Springs); Hudson River Day Line to New York (transfer through New York not included in ticket); Penna. R. R. to Philadelphia. *Rate,* $35.65.

Form 35 (Via Seneca Lake and Thousand Islands; returning via Lakes George and Champlain, Saratoga Springs).—Philad'a & Reading R. R. to Williamsport; Northern Cent. R. W. to Watkins'; Seneca Lake Navigation Co. to Geneva; N. Y. Cent. & Hudson River R. R. to Syracuse; Rome, Watertown & Ogdensburg R. R. to Cape Vincent; Steamer "T. S. Faxton" to Alexandria Bay; Royal Mail Line to Montreal; returning—Grand Trunk R. W. to Rouse's Point; Delaware & Hudson Canal and R. R. to Plattsburg; Champlain Transportation Co. to Fort Ticonderoga; Delaware & Hudson Canal and R. R. to Baldwin; Steamer "Minnehaha" to Caldwell; Stage to Glens Falls; Delaware & Hudson Canal and R. R. to Albany (via Saratoga Springs); Hudson River Day Boats to New York (transfer through New York not included in ticket); Penna. R. R. to Philadelphia. *Rate,* $36.20.

Form 36 (Via Niagara Falls and Thousand Islands; returning via Lake Champlain, Saratoga Springs).—Philad'a & Reading R. R. to Williamsport; Penna. R. R. to Emporium; Buffalo, N. Y. & Philad'a R. R. to Buffalo; Erie R. W. to Niagara Falls; N. Y. Cent. & Hudson River R. R. to Syracuse; Rome, Watertown & Ogdensburg R. R. to Cape Vincent; Steamer "T. S. Faxton" to Alexandria Bay; Royal Mail Line to Montreal; returning—Grand Trunk R. W. to Rouse's Point; Delaware & Hudson Canal and R. R. to Plattsburg; Champlain Transportation Co. to Fort Ticonderoga; Delaware & Hudson Canal and R. R. to Albany (via Saratoga Springs); Hudson River Day Line to New York (transfer through New York not included in ticket); Penna. R. R. to Philadelphia. *Rate,* $36.35.

Form 37 (Via Niagara Falls, Thousand Islands; returning via Lake Champlain, Saratoga Springs).—Philad'a & Reading R. R. to Williamsport; Northern Central R. W. to Elmira; Erie R. W. to Niagara Falls; N. Y. Cent. & Hudson River R. R. to Syracuse; Rome, Watertown & Ogdensburg R. R. to Cape Vincent; Steamer "T. S. Faxton" to Alexandria Bay; Royal Mail Line to Montreal; returning—Grand Trunk R. W. to Rouse's Point; Delaware & Hudson Canal and R. R. to Plattsburg; Champlain Transportation Co. to Fort Ticonderoga; Delaware & Hudson Canal and R. R. to Albany (via Saratoga Springs); Hudson River Day Line to New York (transfer through New York not included in ticket); Penna. R. R. to Philadelphia. *Rate,* $36.35.

MONTREAL, CANADA.—Continued.

Form 38 (Via Saratoga Springs and Thousand Islands, Cayuga Lake, Lakes George and Champlain; returning via Seneca Lake).—Philad'a & Reading R. R. to Allentown; Lehigh Valley R. R. to Sayre; Geneva, Ithaca & Athens R. R. to Ithaca; Cayuga R. R. to Cayuga; N. Y. Cent. & Hudson River R. R. to Schenectady; Delaware & Hudson Canal and R. R. to Glens Falls; Stage to Caldwell; Steamer "Minnehaha" on Lake George to Baldwin; Delaware & Hudson Canal and R. R. to Fort Ticonderoga; Champlain Transportation Co. to Plattsburg; Delaware & Hudson Canal and R. R. to Rouse's Point; Grand Trunk R. W. to Montreal; returning—Royal Mail Line to Alexandria Bay; Steamer "T. S. Faxton" to Cape Vincent; Rome, Watertown & Ogdensburg R. R. to Syracuse; N. Y. Cent. & Hudson River R. R. to Geneva; Seneca Lake Nav. Co. to Watkins'; Northern Cent. R. W. to Williamsport; Philadelphia & Reading R. R. to Philadelphia. *Rate,* $39.85.

Form 41 (Via Seneca Lake, Trenton Falls, and Thousand Islands; returning via Rouse's Point, Saratoga Springs, and New York).—Philad'a & Reading R. R. to Williamsport; Northern Cent. R. W. to Watkins'; Seneca Lake Nav. Co. to Geneva; New York Cent. & Hudson River R. R. to Utica; Utica & Black River R. R. (via Trenton Falls) to Clayton; Steamer "J. H. Kelly" to Alexandria Bay; Royal Mail Line to Montreal; returning—Grand Trunk R. W. to Rouse's Point; Delaware & Hudson Canal and R. R. to Plattsburg; Champlain Transportation Co. to Fort Ticonderoga; Delaware & Hudson Canal and R. R. (via Saratoga Springs) to Albany; Hudson River Day Line to New York (transfer through New York not included in ticket); Penna. R. R. to Philadelphia. *Rate,* $33.40.

Form 42 (Via Seneca Lake, Trenton Falls, and Thousand Islands; returning via Rouse's Point, Lakes Champlain and George, Saratoga Springs, and New York).—Philad'a & Reading R. R. to Williamsport; Northern Cent. R.W. to Watkins'; Seneca Lake Nav. Co. to Geneva; N. Y. Cent. & Hudson River R. R. to Utica; Utica & Black River R. R. (via Trenton Falls) to Clayton; Steamer "J. H. Kelly" to Alexandria Bay; Royal Mail Line to Montreal; returning—Grand Trunk R. W. to Rouse's Point; Delaware & Hudson Canal and R. R. to Plattsburg; Champlain Transportation Co. to Fort Ticonderoga; Delaware & Hudson Canal and R. R. to Baldwin; Steamer "Minnehaha" to Caldwell; Stage to Glens Falls; Delaware & Hudson Canal and R. R. (via Saratoga Springs) to Albany; Hudson River Day Line to New York (transfer through New York not included in ticket); Penna. R. R. to Philadelphia. *Rate,* $36.45.

Form 44 (Via Trenton Falls and Thousand Islands; returning via Lake Champlain and Saratoga Springs).—Philad'a & Reading R. R. to Williamsport; Northern Central R. W. to Canandaigua; N. Y. Cent. & Hudson River R. R. to Utica; Utica & Black River R. R. (via Trenton Falls) to Clayton; Steamer "J. H. Kelly" to Alexandria Bay; Royal Mail Line to Montreal; returning—Grand Trunk R. W. to Rouse's Point; thence via Plattsburg, Lake Champlain, Fort Ticonderoga, Saratoga, Day Line on Hudson River, to New York (transfer through New York not included in ticket); and Penna. R. R. to Philadelphia. *Rate,* $34.00.

Form 45 (Via Trenton Falls and Thousand Islands; returning via Lakes Champlain and George, Fort Ticonderoga, and Saratoga).—Same as Form 44 to Rouse's Point; thence via rail to Plattsburg; Lake Champlain, Fort Ticonderoga; rail to Baldwin; Steamer on Lake George to Caldwell; Stage to Glen's Falls; thence via Saratoga and Day Line on Hudson River to New York (transfer through New York not included in ticket); Penna. R. R. to Philadelphia. *Rate,* $37.05.

MONTREAL, CANADA.—Continued.

Form 46 (Via Cayuga Lake, Saratoga, Lakes George and Champlain; returning via Thousand Islands and Seneca Lake).—Same as Form 38 to Montreal; thence via Royal Mail Line to Alexandria Bay; Steamer "J. H. Kelly" to Clayton; Utica & Black River R. R. (via Trenton Falls) to Utica; N. Y. Cent. & Hudson River R. R. to Geneva; Seneca Lake Nav. Co. to Watkins'; Northern Cent. R. W. to Williamsport; Philad'a & Reading R. R. to Philadelphia.
Rate, $40.15.

Form 47 (Via Niagara Falls, Trenton Falls, and Thousand Islands; returning via Lakes George and Champlain, Saratoga).—Same as Form 36 to Niagara Falls; N. Y. Cent. & Hudson River R. R. to Utica; Utica & Black River R. R. (via Trenton Falls) to Clayton; Steamer "J. H. Kelly" to Alexandria Bay; Royal Mail Line to Montreal; returning as per Form 36.
Rate, $37.75.

Form 48 (Via Niagara Falls and Thousand Islands; returning via Lake George and Saratoga Springs).—Same as Form 37 to Niagara Falls; N. Y. Cent. & Hudson River R. R. to Utica; Utica & Black River R. R. (via Trenton Falls) to Clayton; Steamer "J. H. Kelly" to Alexandria Bay; Royal Mail Line to Montreal; returning as per Form 37.
Rate, $37.75.

Form 71 (Via Thousand Islands, returning via Lake Champlain and Saratoga Springs).—Philad'a & Reading R. R. to Allentown; Lehigh Valley R. R. to Waverly; Erie R. W. to Niagara Falls; N. Y. Cent. & Hudson River R. R. to Syracuse; Rome, Watertown & Ogdensburg R. R. to Cape Vincent; Steamer "T. S. Faxton" to Alexandria Bay; Royal Mail Line to Montreal; returning—Grand Trunk R. W. to Rouse's Point; Delaware & Hudson Canal and R. R. to Plattsburg; Champlain Transportation Co. to Fort Ticonderoga; Delaware & Hudson Canal and R. R. (via Saratoga Springs) to Albany; Hudson River Day Boats to New York (transfer through New York not included in ticket); Penna. R. R. to Philadelphia.
Rate, $36.35.

Form 72 (Via Niagara Falls, Lewiston, and Thousand Islands, returning via Lake Champlain and Saratoga Springs).—Philad'a & Reading R. R., via "Catawissa," to Williamsport; Northern Cent. R. W. to Elmira; Erie R. W. to Niagara Falls; N. Y. Cent. & Hudson River R. R. to Lewiston; Rome, Watertown & Ogdensburg R. R. to Cape Vincent; Steamer "T. S. Faxton" to Alexandria Bay; Royal Mail Line to Montreal; returning—Grand Trunk R. W. to Rouse's Point; Delaware & Hudson Canal and R. R. to Plattsburg; Champlain Transportation Co. to Fort Ticonderoga; Delaware & Hudson Canal and R. R. (via Saratoga Springs) to Albany; Hudson River Day Boats to New York (transfer through New York not included in ticket); Penna. R. R. to Philadelphia.
Rate, $33.75.

Form 73 (Via Niagara Falls, Lewiston, and Thousand Islands, returning via Lake Champlain and Saratoga Springs).—Philad'a & Reading R. R. to Allentown; Lehigh Valley R. R. to Waverly; Erie R. W. to Niagara Falls; N. Y. Cent. & Hudson River R. R. to Lewiston; Rome, Watertown & Ogdensburg R. R. to Cape Vincent; Steamer "T. S. Faxton" to Alexandria Bay; Royal Mail Line to Montreal; returning—Grand Trunk R. W. to Rouse's Point; Delaware & Hudson Canal and R. R. to Plattsburg; Champlain Transportation Co. to Fort Ticonderoga; Delaware & Hudson Canal and R. R. (via Saratoga Springs) to Albany; Hudson River Day Boats to New York (transfer through New York not included in ticket); Penna. R. R. to Philadelphia.
Rate, $33.75.

MONTREAL, CANADA.—Continued.

Form 74 (Via Trenton Falls and Thousand Islands, returning via Lake Champlain and Saratoga Springs).—Philad'a & Reading R. R. to Allentown; Lehigh Valley R. R. to Waverly; Erie R. W. to Elmira; Northern Cent. R. W. to Canandaigua; N. Y. Cent. & Hudson River R. R. to Utica; Utica & Black River R. R. to Clayton; Steamer "J. H. Kelly" to Alexandria Bay; Royal Mail Line to Montreal; returning—Grand Trunk R. W. to Rouse's Point; Delaware & Hudson Canal and R. R. to Plattsburg; Champlain Transportation Co. to Fort Ticonderoga; Delaware & Hudson Canal and R. R. (via Saratoga Springs) to Albany; Hudson River Day Boats to New York (transfer through New York not included in ticket); Penna. R. R. to Philadelphia. *Rate,* $32.60.

Form 75 (Via Thousand Islands, returning via Lake Champlain and Saratoga Springs).—Philad'a & Reading R. R. to Allentown; Lehigh Valley R. R. to Waverly; Erie R. W. to Elmira; Northern Cent. R. W. to Canandaigua; N. Y. Cent. & Hudson River R. R. to Syracuse; Rome, Watertown & Ogdensburg R. R. to Cape Vincent; Steamer "T. S. Faxton" to Alexandria Bay; Royal Mail Line to Montreal; returning—Grand Trunk R. W. to Rouse's Point; Delaware & Hudson Canal and R.R. to Plattsburg; Champlain Transportation Co. to Fort Ticonderoga; Delaware & Hudson Canal and R. R. (via Saratoga Springs) to Albany; Hudson River Day Boats to New York (transfer through New York not included in ticket); Penna. R. R. to Philadelphia. *Rate,* $31.20.

Form 76 (Via Seneca Lake and Thousand Islands, returning via Lake Champlain and Saratoga Springs).—Philad'a & Reading R. R. to Allentown; Lehigh Valley R. R. to Waverly; Erie R. W. to Elmira; Northern Cent. R. W. to Watkins'; Seneca Lake Nav. Co. to Geneva; N. Y. Cent. & Hudson River R. R. to Syracuse; Rome, Watertown & Ogdensburg R. R. to Cape Vincent; Steamer "T. S. Faxton" to Alexandria Bay; Royal Mail Line to Montreal; returning— Grand Trunk R. W. to Rouse's Point; Delaware & Hudson Canal and R. R. to Plattsburg; Champlain Transportation Co. to Fort Ticonderoga; Delaware & Hudson Canal and R. R. (via Saratoga Springs) to Albany; Hudson River Day Boats to New York (transfer through New York not included in ticket); Penna. R. R. to Philadelphia. *Rate,* $31.75.

Form 77 (Via Trenton Falls and Thousand Islands, returning via Lake Champlain and Saratoga Springs).—Philad'a & Reading R. R. to Allentown; Lehigh Valley R. R. to Waverly; Erie R. W. to Niagara Falls; N. Y. Cent. & Hudson River R. R. to Utica; Utica & Black River R. R. to Clayton; Steamer "J. H. Kelly" to Alexandria Bay; Royal Mail Line to Montreal; returning— Grand Trunk R. W. to Rouse's Point; Delaware & Hudson Canal and R. R. to Plattsburg; Champlain Transportation Co. to Fort Ticonderoga; Delaware & Hudson Canal and R. R. (via Saratoga Springs) to Albany; Hudson River Day Boats to New York (transfer through New York not included in ticket); Penna. R. R. to Philadelphia. *Rate,* $37.75.

Form 78 (Via Thousand Islands, returning via Lakes Champlain and George and Saratoga Springs).—Philad'a & Reading R. R. to Allentown; Lehigh Valley R. R. to Elmira; Northern Cent. R. W. to Canandaigua; N. Y.Cent. & Hudson River R. R. to Syracuse; Rome, Watertown & Ogdensburg R. R. to Cape Vincent; Steamer "T. S. Faxton" to Alexandria Bay; Royal Mail Line to Montreal; returning—Grand Trunk R. W. to Rouse's Point; Delaware & Hudson Canal and R. R. to Plattsburg; Champlain Transportation Co. to Fort Ticonderoga; Delaware & Hudson Canal and R. R. to Baldwin; Lake George Steamboat Co. to Caldwell; Glens Falls Stage Co. to Glens Falls; Delaware & Hudson Canal and R. R. (via Saratoga Springs) to Albany; Hudson River Day Boats to New York (transfer through New York not included in ticket); Penna. R. R. to Philadelphia. *Rate,* $35.30.

MONTREAL, CANADA.—Continued.

Form 79 (Via Trenton Falls and Thousand Islands, returning via Lakes George and Champlain and Saratoga Springs).—Philad'a & Reading R. R. to Allentown; Lehigh Valley R. R. to Waverly; Erie R. W. to Elmira; Northern Cent. R. W. to Canandaigua; N. Y. Cent. & Hudson River R. R. to Utica; Utica & Black River R. R. to Clayton; Steamer "J. H. Kelly" to Alexandria Bay; Royal Mail Line to Montreal; returning—Grand Trunk R. W. to Rouse's Point; Delaware & Hudson Canal and R. R. to Plattsburg; Champlain Transportation Co. to Fort Ticonderoga; Delaware & Hudson Canal and R. R. to Baldwin; Lake George Steamboat Co. to Caldwell; Glens Falls Stage Co. to Glens Falls; Delaware & Hudson Canal and R. R. (via Saratoga Springs) to Albany; Hudson River Day Boats to New York (transfer through New York not included in ticket); Penna. R. R. to Philadelphia.   *Rate,* $36.75.

Form 80 (Via Seneca Lake and Thousand Islands, returning via Lakes Champlain and George and Saratoga Springs).—Philad'a & Reading R. R. to Allentown; Lehigh Valley R. R. to Waverly; Erie R. W. to Elmira; Northern Cent. R. W. to Watkins'; Seneca Lake Nav. Co. to Geneva; N. Y. Cent. & Hudson River R. R. to Syracuse; Rome, Watertown & Ogdensburg R. R. to Cape Vincent; Steamer "T. S. Faxton" to Alexandria Bay; Royal Mail Line to Montreal; returning—Grand Trunk R. W. to Rouse's Point; Delaware & Hudson Canal and R. R. to Plattsburg; Champlain Transportation Co. to Fort Ticonderoga; Delaware & Hudson Canal and R. R. to Baldwin; Lake George Steamboat Co. to Caldwell; Glens Falls Stage Co. to Glens Falls; Delaware & Hudson Canal and R. R. (via Saratoga Springs) to Albany; Hudson River Day Boats to New York (transfer through New York not included in ticket); Penna. R. R. to Philadelphia.   *Rate,* $34.80.

NIAGARA FALLS.

The following NINE FORMS TO NIAGARA FALLS, N. Y., are used only in connection WITH ROUTES BEYOND THAT POINT via LAKE ONTARIO and RIVER ST. LAWRENCE, or via GRAND TRUNK RAILWAY, and are given in order that passengers may have a choice of nine routes from Philadelphia to Niagara Falls (rates are included in rate for routes mentioned):—

Form F—9.—Philad'a & Reading R. R. to Harrisburg; Northern Cent. R. W to Sunbury; Penna. R. R. to Williamsport; Northern Cent. R. W. to Canandaigua; N. Y. Cent. & Hudson River R. R. to Niagara Falls.

Form F—10.—Philad'a & Reading R. R. to Williamsport; Northern Cent. R. W. to Canandaigua; N. Y. Cent. & Hudson River R. R. to Niagara Falls.

Form F—137.—Philad'a & Reading R. R. to Harrisburg; Northern Cent. R. W. to Sunbury; Penna. R. R. to Williamsport; Northern Cent. R. W. to Elmira; Erie R. W. to Niagara Falls.

Form F—138.—Philad'a & Reading R. R. to Williamsport; Northern Cent. R. W. to Elmira; Erie R. W. to Niagara Falls.

Form F—188.—Philad'a & Reading R. R. to Allentown; Lehigh Valley R. R. to Waverly; Erie R. W. to Niagara Falls.

Form F—197.—Philad'a & Reading R. R. to Allentown; Lehigh Valley R. R. to Waverly; Erie R. W. to Elmira; Northern Cent. R. W. to Canandaigua; N. Y. Cent. & Hudson River R. R. to Niagara Falls.

Form F—198.—Philad'a & Reading R. R. to Williamsport; Northern Cent. R. W. to Watkins'; Seneca Lake Nav. Co. to Geneva; N. Y. Cent. & Hudson River R. R. to Niagara Falls.

43

43

NIAGARA FALLS, N. Y.—Continued.

Form F—244.—Philad'a & Reading R. R. to Williamsport; Penna. R. R. to Emporium; Buffalo, New York & Philad'a R. R. to Buffalo; Erie R. W. to Niagara Falls.

Form F—260.—Philad'a & Reading R. R. to Harrisburg; Northern Cent. R. W. to Sunbury; Penna. R. R. to Emporium; Erie R. W. to Niagara Falls.

NIAGARA FALLS, N. Y., AND RETURN.

Form Sp. Exc.—1.—Philad'a & Reading R. R., via "Catawissa," to Williamsport; Northern Cent. R. W. to Elmira; Erie R. W. to Niagara Falls; returning same route. *Rate,* $17.50.

Form Sp. Exc.—2.—Same as No. 1, returning to Elmira; Leh. Val. R. R. to Allentown; Philad'a & Reading R. R. to Philadelphia. *Rate,* $19.50.

Form Sp. Exc.—3.—Same as No. 1 to Niagara Falls; returning—Erie R. W. to Elmira; Northern Cent. R. W. to Williamsport; Penna. R. R. to Sunbury; Northern Cent. R. W. to Harrisburg; Philad'a & Reading R. R. to Philadelphia. *Rate,* $19.50.

Form Sp. Exc.—4.—Philad'a & Reading R. R., via "Catawissa," to Williamsport; Northern Cent. R. W. to Canandaigua; N. Y. Cent. & Hudson River R. R. to Niagara Falls; returning same route. *Rate,* $17.50.

Form Sp. Exc.—4½.—Philad'a & Reading R. R. to Williamsport; Northern Cent. R. W. to Watkins'; Seneca Lake Nav. Co. to Geneva; N. Y. Cent. & Hudson River R. R. to Niagara Falls, via Rochester; returning—N. Y. Cent. & Hudson River R. R. to Canandaigua; Northern Cent. R. W. to Williamsport; Philad'a & Reading R. R. to Philadelphia. *Rate,* $18.00.

Form Sp. Exc.—5.—Same as No. 4 to Niagara Falls; returning same route to Williamsport; thence via Penna. R. R. to Sunbury; Northern Cent. R. W. to Harrisburg; Philadelphia & Reading R. R. to Philadelphia. *Rate,* $19.50.

Form Sp. Exc.—6.—Philad'a & Reading R. R. to Harrisburg; Northern Cent. R. W. to Sunbury; Penna. R. R. to Williamsport; Northern Cent. R. W. to Canandaigua; N. Y. Cent. & Hudson River R. R. to Niagara Falls, via Rochester; returning same route to Williamsport; thence via "Catawissa" and Philad'a & Reading R. R. to Philadelphia. *Rate,* $19.50.

Form Sp. Exc.—7.—Philad'a & Reading R. R. to Harrisburg; Northern Cent. R. W. to Sunbury; Penna. R. R. to Williamsport; Northern Cent. R. W. to Canandaigua; N. Y. Cent. & Hudson River R. R. to Niagara Falls, via Rochester; returning same route. *Rate,* $17.50.

Form Sp. Exc.—8.—Philad'a & Reading R. R. to Harrisburg; Northern Cent. R. W. to Sunbury; Pennsylvania R. R. to Williamsport; Northern Cent. R. W. to Elmira; Erie R.W. to Niagara Falls; returning same route. *Rate,* $17.50.

Form Sp. Exc.—9.—Philadelphia & Reading R. R. to Allentown; Lehigh Valley R. R. to Waverly; Erie R. W. to Niagara Falls; returning same route. *Rate,* $17.50.

NIAGARA FALLS, N. Y., AND RETURN.—Continued.

Form 7—A.—Philad'a & Reading R. R., via "Catawissa," to Williamsport; Northern Cent. R. W. to Elmira; Erie R. W. to Niagara Falls; returning— N.Y. Cent. & Hudson River R. R. to Albany; Hudson River Day Boats ("D. Drew" or "C. Vibbard") to New York (transfer through New York not included in ticket); Penna. R. R. to Philadelphia.   *Rate,* $20.00.

Form 8.—Philad'a & Reading R. R., via "Catawissa," to Williamsport; Northern Cent. R. W. to Elmira; Erie R. W. to Niagara Falls; returning— N. Y. Cent. & Hudson River R. R. to Albany; Hudson River Day Boats ("D. Drew" or "C. Vibbard") to New York (transfer through New York not included in ticket); N. J. Cent. R. R. to Easton; Leh. Val. R. R. to Allentown; Philad'a & Reading R. R. to Philadelphia.   *Rate,* $21.00.

Form 11.—Philad'a & Reading R. R., via "Catawissa," to Williamsport; Northern Cent. R. W. to Watkins'; Seneca Lake Navigation Co. to Geneva; N. Y. Cent. & Hudson River R. R. to Niagara Falls; returning—Erie R. W. to Elmira; Northern Cent. R. W. to Williamsport; Penna. R. R. to Sunbury; Northern Cent. R. W. to Harrisburg; Penna. R. R. to Philadelphia.   *Rate,* $19.50.

Form 12.—Philad'a & Reading R. R. to Harrisburg; Northern Cent. R. W. to Sunbury; Penna. R. R. to Williamsport; Northern Cent. R. W. to Watkins'; Seneca Lake Navigation Co. to Geneva; N. Y. Cent. & Hudson River R. R. to Niagara Falls; returning—Erie R. W. to Elmira; Northern Cent. R. W. to Williamsport; Philad'a & Reading R. R. to Philadelphia.   *Rate,* $19.50.

Form 14.—Philad'a & Reading R. R., via "Catawissa," to Williamsport; Northern Cent. R. W. to Watkins'; Seneca Lake Navigation Co. to Geneva; N. Y. Cent. & Hudson River R. R. to Niagara Falls and return to Canandaigua; Northern Cent. R. W. to Williamsport; Penna. R. R. to Sunbury; Northern Cent. R. W. to Harrisburg; Penna. R. R. to Philadelphia.   *Rate,* $19.50.

Form 14—A—1.—Philad'a & Reading R. R., via "Catawissa," to Williamsport; Northern Cent. R. W. to Watkins'; Seneca Lake Navigation Co. to Geneva; N. Y. Cent. & Hudson River R. R. to Niagara Falls and return to Albany; Hudson River Day Boats to New York (transfer through New York not included in ticket); Penna. R. R. to Philadelphia.   *Rate,* $20.00.

Form 14—B—1.—Philad'a & Reading R. R. to Harrisburg; Northern Cent. R. W. to Sunbury; Penna. R. R. to Williamsport; Northern Cent. R. W. to Watkins'; Seneca Lake Navigation Co. to Geneva; N. Y. Cent. & Hudson River R. R. to Niagara Falls and return to Albany; Hudson River Day Boats to New York (transfer through New York not included in ticket); Penna. R. R. to Philadelphia.   *Rate,* $20.00.

Form 20.—Philad'a & Reading R. R. to Allentown; Leh. Val. R. R. to Easton; Cent. R. R. of N. J. to New York (transfer through New York not included in ticket); Hudson River Day Boats ("D. Drew" or "C. Vibbard") to Albany; N. Y. Cent. & Hudson River R. R. to Niagara Falls; returning—Erie R. W. to Elmira; Northern Cent. R. W. to Williamsport; Philad'a & Reading R. R. to Philadelphia.   *Rate,* $21.00.

Form 21.—Penna. R. R. to New York (transfer through New York not included in ticket); Hudson River Day Boats ("D. Drew" or "C. Vibbard") to Albany; N. Y. Cent. & Hudson River R. R. to Niagara Falls; returning—Erie R. W. to Elmira; Northern Cent. R. W. to Williamsport; Philad'a & Reading R. R. to Philadelphia.   *Rate,* $20.00.

45

NIAGARA FALLS, N. Y., AND RETURN.—Continued.

Form 22.—Penna. R. R. to New York (transfer through New York not included in ticket); Hudson River Day Boats ("D. Drew" or "C. Vibbard") to Albany; N. Y. Cent. & Hudson River R. R. to Niagara Falls; returning—N. Y. Cent. R. R. to Canandaigua, via Rochester; Northern Cent. R. W. (via Watkins' Glen, with privilege of stopping off) to Williamsport; Penna. R. R. to Sunbury; Northern Cent. R. W. to Harrisburg; Philad'a & Reading R. R. to Philadelphia. *Rate,* $20.00.

Form 30.—Philad'a & Reading R. R. to Williamsport; Penna. R. R. to Emporium; Buffalo, N. Y. & Philad'a R. R. to Buffalo; Erie R. W. to Niagara Falls; returning—N. Y. Cent. & Hudson River R. R. to Albany; Hudson River Day Boats to New York (transfer through New York not included in ticket); Penna. R. R. to Philadelphia. *Rate,* $20.00.

Form 31.—Philad'a & Reading R. R. to Williamsport; Penna. R. R. to Emporium; Buffalo, N. Y. & Philad'a R. R. to Buffalo; Erie R. W. to Niagara Falls; returning—Erie R. W. to Elmira; Northern Cent. R. W. to Williamsport; Philad'a & Reading R. R. to Philadelphia. *Rate,* $19.50.

Form 50.—Philad'a & Reading R. R. to Allentown; Lehigh Valley R. R. to Waverly; Erie R. W. to Niagara Falls; returning—N. Y. Cent. & Hudson River R. R. to Albany; Hudson River Day Boats to New York (transfer through New York not included in ticket); Penna. R. R. to Philadelphia. *Rate,* $20.00.

Form 51.—Philad'a & Reading R. R., via "Catawissa," to Williamsport; Northern Cent. R. W. to Watkins'; Seneca Lake Nav. Co. to Geneva; N. Y. Cent. & Hudson River R. R. to Niagara Falls; returning—Erie R. W. to Waverly; Lehigh Valley R. R. to Allentown; Philad'a & Reading R. R. to Allentown. *Rate,* $19.50.

Form 52.—Philad'a & Reading R. R. to Allentown; Lehigh Valley R. R. to Waverly; Erie R. W. to Elmira; Northern Cent. R. W. to Watkins'; Seneca Lake Nav. Co. to Geneva; N. Y. Cent. & Hudson River R. R. to Niagara Falls; returning—Erie R. W. to Elmira; Northern Cent. R. W. to Williamsport; Philad'a & Reading R. R. to Philadelphia. *Rate,* $19.50.

Form 53.—Philad'a & Reading R. R. to Allentown; Lehigh Valley R. R. to Waverly; Erie R. W. to Elmira; Northern Cent. R. W. to Watkins'; Seneca Lake Nav. Co. to Geneva; N. Y. Cent. & Hudson River R. R. to Niagara Falls and return to Albany; Hudson River Day Boats to New York (transfer through New York not included in ticket); Penna. R. R. to Philadelphia. *Rate,* $20.00.

Form 54.—Penna. R. R. to New York (transfer through New York not included in ticket); Hudson River Day Boats to Albany; N. Y. Cent. & Hudson River R. R. to Niagara Falls; returning—Erie R. W. to Waverly; Lehigh Valley R. R. to Allentown; Philad'a & Reading R. R. to Philadelphia. *Rate,* $20.00.

Form 55.—Penna. R. R. to New York (transfer through New York not included in ticket); Hudson River Day Boats to Albany; N. Y. Cent. & Hudson River R. R. to Niagara Falls and return to Canandaigua; Northern Cent. R. W. to Elmira; Erie R. W. to Waverly; Lehigh Valley R. R. to Allentown; Philad'a & Reading R. R. to Philadelphia. *Rate,* $20.00.

Form 61.—Philad'a & Reading R. R. to Allentown; Lehigh Valley R. R. to Waverly; Erie R. W. to Niagara Falls; returning—N. Y. Cent. and Hudson River R. R. to Canandaigua; Northern Cent. R. W. to Elmira; Erie R. W. to Waverly; Lehigh Valley R. R. to Allentown; Philad'a & Reading R. R. to Philadelphia.   *Rate,* $19.50.

Form 62.—Philad'a & Reading R. R., via "Catawissa," to Williamsport; Northern Cent. R. W. to Elmira; Erie R. W. to Niagara Falls; returning— N. Y. Cent. & Hudson River R. R. to Charlotte; Rome, Watertown & Ogdensburg R. R. to Sterling; Southern Cent. R. R. to State Line; Lehigh Valley R. R. to Allentown; Philad'a & Reading R. R. to Philadelphia.   *Rate,* $19.50.

Form 63.—Philad'a & Reading R. R., via "Catawissa," to Williamsport; Northern Cent. R. W. to Elmira; Erie R. W. to Niagara Falls; returning—N. Y. Cent. & Hudson River R. R. to Cayuga; Cayuga R. R. to Ithaca; Utica, Ithaca & Elmira R. R. to Elmira; Erie R. W. to Waverly; Lehigh Valley R. R. to Allentown; Philad'a & Reading R. R. to Philadelphia.   *Rate,* $20.00.

Form 64.—Philad'a & Reading R. R., via "Catawissa," to Williamsport; Northern Cent. R. W. to Elmira; Erie R. W. to Niagara Falls; returning—N. Y. Cent. & Hudson River R. R. to Cayuga; Cayuga R. R. to Ithaca; Utica, Ithaca & Elmira R. R. to Elmira; Northern Cent. R. W. to Williamsport; Philad'a & Reading R. R. to Philadelphia.   *Rate,* $20.30.

CHOICE OF NINE ROUTES TO NIAGARA FALLS—FORMS F—9, 10, 137, 138, 188, 197, 198, 244, 260.   Page 15.

Form X—11 (Via Quebec and Portland).—Choice of nine routes to Niagara Falls; thence to Lewiston, to Toronto, to Kingston, to Prescott, to Montreal, to Quebec, to Portland; Portland to Boston via rail; Sound lines to New York, and Penna. R. R. to Philadelphia.   *Rate,* $41.75.

Form X—12 (Via Montreal and St. John's).—Choice of nine routes to Niagara Falls; thence to Lewiston, to Toronto, to Kingston, to Prescott, to Montreal, to St. John's, to Burlington, via Bellows Falls and Fitchburg to Boston; Sound lines to New York, and Penna. R. R. to Philadelphia.   *Rate,* $38.75.

Form X—15 (Via Montreal and Portland).—Choice of nine routes to Niagara Falls; thence to Lewiston, Toronto, and Montreal; thence to Portland (via Gorham); thence via rail or steamer to Boston; Sound lines to New York, and Penna. R. R. to Philadelphia.   *Rate,* $38.75.

Form X—16 (Via Montreal, St. John's, and Vt. Cent. R. R.).—Choice of nine routes to Niagara Falls; thence to Lewiston, Toronto, and Montreal; thence via St. John's and Vt. Cent. R. R. to White River Junction; thence via Concord and Nashua to Boston; Sound lines to New York, and Penna. R. R. to Philadelphia.   *Rate,* $38.75.

Form X—18.—Choice of nine routes to Niagara Falls; thence to Lewiston, Toronto, and Montreal; thence via Rouse's Point, Fort Ticonderoga, Lake George, and Glen's Falls to Saratoga Springs; Rens. & Sara. R. R. to Albany; Day or Night Boats to New York; Penna. R. R. to Philadelphia. (Via rail from Albany to New York, rate is 85 cents additional.)   *Rate,* $39.95.

NIAGARA FALLS, N. Y., AND RETURN.—Continued.

Form S X—19.—Choice of nine routes to Niagara Falls; thence to Lewiston, Toronto, and Montreal; thence via Rouse's Point, Lake Champlain, Fort Ticonderoga, Lake George, Glen's Falls, and Saratoga Springs to Troy; New York Central & Hudson River R. R. to New York; Penna. R. R. to Philadelphia. *Rate,* $41.25.

Form X—20.—Same as Form X—19 to Glen's Falls; thence to Albany; People's Night Line of Steamers to New York; Penna. R. R. to Philadelphia. *Rate,* $40.25.

Form S X—21.—Choice of nine routes to Niagara Falls; thence to Lewiston, Toronto, and Montreal; thence to Rouse's Point; thence via Lake Champlain Steamers to Whitehall; Rens. & Sara. R. R. to Troy; New York Central & Hudson River R. R. to New York; Penna. R. R. to Philadelphia. *Rate,* $38.25.

Form X—22.—Choice of nine routes to Niagara Falls; thence to Lewiston, Toronto, and Montreal; thence via Rouse's Point, Lake Champlain, and Whitehall to Albany, and via People's Night Line of Steamers to New York; Penna. R. R. to Philadelphia. *Rate,* $37.25.

Form X—23 (Via Montreal and Lake Champlain).—Same as Form X—18 to Montreal; thence via Rouse's Point and Lake Champlain to Whitehall; rail to Saratoga Springs; Rens. & Sara. R. R. to Albany; Day or Night Boats to New York; Penna. R. R. to Philadelphia. (Via rail from Albany to New York, rate is 85 cents additional.) *Rate,* $36.95.

Form X—24.—Choice of nine routes to Niagara Falls; thence via Lewiston, Toronto, and Montreal; thence via White Mountains to Portland; thence via Boston to Providence or Fall River; and Stonington or Newport; and Sound Steamers to New York; Penna. R. R. to Philadelphia. *Rate,* $38.75.

Form X—25.—Choice of nine routes to Niagara Falls; thence to Lewiston, Toronto, Montreal, and Quebec; Quebec to Portland (via White Mountains); Portland to Boston; thence to Providence or Fall River; and Stonington or Newport; Sound Steamers to New York; Penna. R. R. to Philadelphia. *Rate,* $41.75.

Form X—26.—Choice of nine routes to Niagara Falls; thence to Lewiston, Toronto, and Montreal; thence to Rouse's Point; Lake Champlain Steamers to Fort Ticonderoga; thence via Lake George, Glen's Falls, and Saratoga to Albany; Hudson River Day Line of Steamers to New York; Penna. R. R. to Philadelphia. *Rate,* $40.25.

Form X—27.—Choice of nine routes to Niagara Falls; thence to Lewiston, Toronto, and Montreal; thence to Rouse's Point; Lake Champlain Steamers to Whitehall; thence to Albany; thence via Hudson River Day Line of Steamers to New York; Penna. R. R. to Philadelphia. *Rate,* $37.25.

Form X—28 (Via White Mountains).—Same as Form X—18 to Montreal; Grand Trunk R. W., Montreal to Alpine House (Gorham); thence via stages to Glen and Tip-Top Houses; thence via rail to Base; Crawford, Fabyan, and Profile Houses; thence via Littleton and Wells River to White River Junction; thence via Burlington, Ticonderoga, and Baldwin; Lake George to Caldwell; stage to Glen's Falls; Rens. & Sara. R. R. to Saratoga Springs; Rens. & Sara. R. R. to Albany; Day or Night Boats to New York; Penna. R. R. to Philadelphia. (Via rail from Albany to New York, rate is 85 cents additional.) *Rate,* $65.45.

Form X—29.—Choice of nine routes to Niagara Falls; thence via Lewiston and Toronto to Montreal; thence to Rouse's Point; thence via Lake Champlain to White Hall; thence to Saratoga, to Rutland, to Bellows Falls, to Fitchburg, to Boston; Sound Lines to New York; Penna. R. R. to Philadelphia. *Rate,* $44.25.

Form X—30.—Choice of nine routes to Niagara Falls; thence to Lewiston, Toronto, and Montreal; thence via Grand Trunk R.W. or Richelieu Line of Steamers to Quebec (meals and berths extra); thence to Littleton via Sherbrooke and Wells River; thence via stages to Profile, Fabyan, and Crawford Houses; thence to Mount Washington; thence via rail to Summit; thence via stages to Gorham; thence via Grand Trunk R. W. to Portland, and Boston & Maine or Eastern R. R. to Boston; Sound lines to New York, and Penna. R. R. to Philadelphia.
Rate, $60.75.

Form X—31.—Choice of nine routes to Niagara Falls; thence via Lewiston and Toronto; thence to Quebec, Sherbrooke, Lake Memphremagog, Wells River, Profile, Fabyan, and Crawford Houses; thence to Mt. Washington, Glen House, and Gorham; rail to Portland; rail or steamer to Boston; Sound Steamers to New York; Penna. R. R. to Philadelphia. *Rate,* $62.25.

Form X—34 (Via Montreal, Lake Champlain, Saratoga, and New York)—Choice of nine routes to Niagara Falls; thence to Lewiston, Toronto, and Montreal; thence via Rouse's Point to Lake Champlain, to Lake George, to Albany (via Saratoga Springs); People's Line Steamers to New York; Sound lines to Boston; Sound lines to New York, and Penna. R. R. to Philadelphia.
Rate, $49.25.

Form X—35 (Via White Mountains).—Choice of nine routes to Niagara Falls; thence to Lewiston, Toronto, Prescott, and Montreal; thence to St. John's, White River Junction, Wells River, Littleton, Profile, Fabyan, and Crawford Houses; rail via Concord and Nashua to Boston; Sound lines to New York, and Penna. R. R. to Philadelphia. *Rate,* $49.75.

Form X—36.—Choice of nine routes to Niagara Falls; thence via Lewiston and Toronto to Montreal; thence to Quebec; thence via Grand Trunk R. W. to Gorham; thence via Stages to Glen and Tip-Top Houses; thence via rail to Base; Stages to Crawford, Fabyan, and Profile Houses; thence to Littleton via stage; thence to Boston via Concord and Nashua; thence to Newport via Providence or Fall River; Sound Steamers to New York; Penna. R. R. to Philadelphia.
Rate, $63.75.

Form S X—37.—Choice of nine routes to Niagara Falls; thence to Lewiston, Toronto, Montreal, and Quebec; thence via Sherbrooke and Newport to Wells River; thence via Littleton to Profile, Fabyan, and Crawford Houses to Concord; thence to Boston via Nashua; thence to Providence or Fall River and Stonington or Newport; Sound Steamers to New York; Penna. R. R. to Philadelphia.
Rate, $54.25.

Form X—38 (Via Montreal, Rouse's Point, and Lake Champlain).—Choice of nine routes to Niagara Falls; thence to Lewiston, Toronto, and Montreal; thence via Rouse's Point to Burlington via Lake Champlain; thence via Bellows Falls, to Fitchburg, and Boston via rail; Sound lines to New York, and Penna. R. R. to Philadelphia. *Rate,* $40.25.

Form X—39.—Choice of nine routes to Niagara Falls; thence via Lewiston and Toronto to Kingston; thence to Prescott and Ogdensburg, to Moers' Junction, to Plattsburg (Fouquet's Hotel), to Burlington, to Bellows Falls, to Fitchburg, to Boston; Sound lines to New York; Penna. R. R. to Philadelphia.
Rate, $35.25.

Form X—42.—Choice of nine routes to Niagara Falls; thence via Lewiston and Toronto to Montreal; Grand Trunk R. W. to St. John's; Vt. Cent. R. R. to Burlington; thence to Whitehall; Rens. & Sara R. R. to Albany; Hudson River Day Line of Steamers to New York; Penna. R. R. to Philadelphia.
Rate, $36.75.

Form X—43.—Same as Form X—42 to Burlington; thence via Fort Ticon-
deroga, Lake George, and Caldwell to Glen's Falls; Rens. & Sara. R. R. to
Albany; Hudson River Day Boats to New York; Penna. R. R. to Philadelphia.
Rate, $39.75.

Form X—46.—Same as Form X—42 to Burlington; thence via Bellows Falls
to Brattleboro; thence to South Vernon; Conn. Riv. R. R. to Springfield; New
York, New Haven & Hartford R. R. (via New Haven) to New York; Penna. R. R.
to Philadelphia. *Rate*, $35.75.

Form X—52.—Same as Form X—18 to Montreal; thence via rail to St. John's
and Burlington; Champlain Transfer Co. to Whitehall; Rens. & Sara. R. R. to
Saratoga Springs; Rens. & Sara. R. R. to Albany; Day or Night Boats to New
York; Penna. R. R. to Philadelphia. (Via rail from Albany to New York, rate
is 85 cents additional.) *Rate*, $36.70.

Form X—53.—Same as Form X—18 to Montreal; thence to St. John's and
Burlington; thence via Ticonderoga, Lake George, and Caldwell's to Glen's
Falls; Rens. & Sara. R. R. to Saratoga Springs; Rens. & Sara. R. R. to Albany;
Day or Night Boats to New York; Penna. R. R. to Philadelphia. (Via rail from
Albany to New York, rate is 85 cents additional.) *Rate*, $39.45.

Form X—136.—Choice of nine routes to Niagara Falls; thence to Lewiston,
Toronto, and Montreal; thence to Sherbrooke; Conn. & Pass. Rivers R. R. to
White River Junction; Northern R. R. to Concord; Concord R. R. to Nashua;
Boston, Lowell & Nashua R. R. to Boston; Sound lines to New York, and Penna.
R. R. to Philadelphia. *Rate*, $39.75.

Form X—137.—Choice of nine routes to Niagara Falls; thence to Lewiston,
Toronto, Montreal, and Quebec; thence to Sherbrooke; thence same as Form X—
136 to Boston; Sound lines to New York, and Penna. R. R. to Philadelphia.
Rate, $42.75.

Form X—138.—Choice of nine routes to Niagara Falls; thence to Lewiston,
Toronto, Montreal, and Sherbrooke to White River Junction; Vt. Cent. R. R. to .
South Vernon; Conn. Riv. R. R. to Springfield; New York, New Haven & Hart-
ford R. R. to New York; Penna. R. R. to Philadelphia. *Rate*, $36.75.

Form X—139.—Same as Form X—138 to Montreal; thence via Quebec;
thence to Sherbrooke; thence as Form X—138 to New York; Penna. R. R. to
Philadelphia. *Rate*, $39.75.

Form X—140.—Same as Form X—138 via Montreal to Sherbrooke; thence
to White River Junction, Concord, and Nashua to Boston; thence via Providence,
or Fall River to Stonington or Newport; thence via Sound Steamers to New
York; Penna. R. R. to Philadelphia. *Rate*, $40.00.

Form X—141 (Via Quebec, Sherbrooke, &c.).—Choice of nine routes to
Niagara Falls; thence to Lewiston, Toronto, and Montreal; thence to Quebec;
thence via Sherbrooke, White River Junction, Concord, Nashua, Boston, and
Sound Steamers to New York; Penna. R. R. to Philadelphia. *Rate*, $43.25.

Form X—142.—Choice of nine routes to Niagara Falls; thence to Lewiston,
Toronto, and Montreal; thence via Grand Trunk R. W. to Northumberland;
thence via Boston, Concord & Montreal and White Mountains R. R.'s to Concord;
thence via Concord & Nashua to Boston; Sound lines to New York, and Penna.
R. R. to Philadelphia. *Rate*, $40.75.

NIAGARA FALLS, N. Y., AND RETURN.—Continued.

Form X—144.—Choice of nine routes to Niagara Falls; thence to Lewiston, Toronto, and Montreal; thence to Northumberland, Concord, and Nashua; thence via Worcester & Nashua R. R. to Worcester; Boston, Hartford & Erie R. R. to New London; Norwich Steamboat to New York; Penna. R. R. to Philadelphia.
Rate, $41.00.

Form X—145.—Choice of nine routes to Niagara Falls; thence to Lewiston, Toronto, and Montreal; thence to Quebec via Grand Trunk R. W. or Richelieu Steamers; thence to Northumberland; thence same as Form X—142 to Boston; Sound lines to New York, and Penna. R. R. to Philadelphia. *Rate,* $43.75.

Form X—147.—Choice of nine routes to Niagara Falls; thence via Lewiston and Toronto to Montreal; thence via Groveton to Fabyan and Profile Houses; thence to Littleton; thence via Plymouth, Concord, and Nashua to Boston; Sound lines to New York, and Penna. R. R. to Philadelphia. *Rate,* $48.50.

Form X—148.—Choice of nine routes to Niagara Falls; thence via Lewiston and Toronto to Montreal; thence to Groveton, Fabyan House, Bethlehem; stages to Profile House and Littleton; thence to Nashua; thence to Worcester; thence to Allen's Point; thence via steamer to New York; Penna. R. R. to Philadelphia.
Rate, $46.50.

Form X—149.—Same as Form X—148 to Nashua; thence to West Concord; thence to Weir Junction; thence to Mansfield; thence to Newport; Sound Steamers to New York; Penna. R. R. to Philadelphia. *Rate,* $46.50.

Form X—150.—Choice of nine routes to Niagara Falls; thence to Lewiston and Toronto to Montreal; thence via Grand Trunk R. W. to Northumberland; thence to Concord, Nashua, Lowell, and Mansfield; thence to Weir Junction; thence via Fall River or Newport to New York; Penna. R. R. to Philadelphia.
Rate, $41.00.

Form X—154.—Choice of nine routes to Niagara Falls; thence via Lewiston and Toronto to Montreal; thence to Gorham; stage to Glen House; stage to Summit; Mt. Washington R. R. to Base; stage to Fabyan House; thence to Bethlehem; thence to Profile House; thence to Littleton; thence to Boston via Concord and Nashua; Sound lines to New York, and Penna. R. R. to Philadelphia.
Rate, $58.25.

Form X—183.—Choice of nine routes to Niagara Falls; thence via Lewiston and Toronto to Montreal; thence via Rouse's Point, Burlington, Montpelier, Wells River, Concord, and Nashua to Boston; Sound Steamers to New York; Penna. R. R. to Philadelphia. *Rate,* $43.00.

Form X—184.—Same as Form X 183 to Montreal; thence to St. John's, West Farnham, Newport, Wells River, Concord, and Nashua to Boston; Sound Steamers to New York; Penna. R. R. to Philadelphia. *Rate,* $38.75.

Form X—185.—Choice of nine routes to Niagara Falls; thence via Lewiston, Toronto, Kingston, and Prescott to Montreal; thence via Rouse's Point, Burlington, Bellows Falls, South Vernon, Springfield, and New Haven to New York; Penna. R. R. to Philadelphia. *Rate,* $39.00.

Form X—186.—Choice of nine routes to Niagara Falls; thence via Lewiston, Toronto, Kingston, Prescott, and Montreal to Quebec; thence to Alpine House (Gorham); stage to Glen and Tip-Top Houses; rail to Base; stage to Crawford House; rail to Fabyan's and return to Crawford House; thence to Bethlehem; stage to Profile House and Littleton; thence via Wells River, Montpelier, and Burlington; "Lake Champlain" to Fort Ticonderoga; thence via Baldwin, "Lake George," and Glens Falls to Albany; Day Line of Steamers to New York; Penna. R. R. to Philadelphia. *Rate,* $66.25.

...

NIAGARA FALLS, N. Y., AND RETURN.—Continued.

Form X—188.—Same as Form X 186 to Quebec; thence via Sherbrooke, Wells River, and Montpelier to Burlington; "Lake Champlain" to Fort Ticonderoga; rail to Baldwin; "Lake George" to Caldwell; stage to Glens Falls; rail to Albany; Hudson River Day Boats to New York; Penna. R. R. to Philadelphia. *Rate,* $48.25.

Form X—189.—Same as Form X 188 to Albany; People's Line of Steamers to New York; Penna. R. R. to Philadelphia. *Rate,* $48.25.

Form X—190.—Choice of nine routes to Niagara Falls; thence via Lewiston, Toronto, and Montreal to Quebec; thence via Sherbrooke and Wells River to Littleton; stage to Profile House and Bethlehem; rail to Crawford House and return to Fabyan; thence via Wells River, White River Junction, South Vernon, Springfield, and New Haven to New York; Penna. R. R. to Philadelphia. *Rate,* $53.75.

Form X—191.—Choice of nine routes to Niagara Falls; thence via Lewiston, Toronto, Kingston, and Prescott to Montreal; thence to Alpine House (Gorham), Glen, and Tip-Top Houses; rail to Base; Fabyan House and Bethlehem; stage to Profile House and Littleton; rail via Plymouth, Concord, and Nashua to Boston; thence via Providence or Fall River to Stonington or Newport; Sound Steamers to New York; Penna. R. R. to Philadelphia. *Rate,* $59.25.

Form X—192.—Choice of nine routes to Niagara Falls; thence via Lewiston, Toronto, Kingston, and Prescott to Montreal; thence to Groveton, Fabyan, Mt. Washington, and Summit; stage to Glen House and North Conway; rail to Boston; thence via Providence or Fall River to Stonington or Newport; Sound Steamers to New York; Penna. R. R. to Philadelphia. *Rate,* $53.25.

Form X—194.—Choice of nine routes to Niagara Falls; thence via Lewiston, Toronto, Kingston, and Prescott to Montreal; thence to Sherbrooke, Wells River, Littleton, Profile House, Bethlehem, and Fabyan; stage to Crawford House and return to Fabyan; thence via Concord and Nashua to Boston; Providence or Fall River to Stonington or Newport; Sound Steamers to New York; Penna. R. R. to Philadelphia. *Rate,* $52.75.

Form X—195.—Choice of nine routes to Niagara Falls; thence via Lewiston, Toronto, and Montreal to Quebec; thence to Alpine House (Gorham), Glen and Tip-Top Houses; thence via Portland to Boston; Providence or Fall River to Stonington or Newport; Sound Steamers to New York; Penna. R. R. to Philadelphia. *Rate,* $53.25.

Form X—196.—Choice of nine routes to Niagara Falls; thence via Lewiston and Toronto to Montreal; thence via St. John's, West Farnham, Newport, Wells River, and Littleton; stage to Profile House and Bethlehem; rail via Fabyan and Portland to Boston; thence via Newport or Stonington and Sound Steamers to New York; Penna. R. R. to Philadelphia. *Rate,* $49.25.

Form X—197.—Choice of nine routes to Niagara Falls; thence via Lewiston and Toronto to Montreal; thence via Sherbrooke, Wells River, and Littleton; stage to Profile House and Bethlehem; rail to Fabyan, North Conway, and via Providence or Fall River to Stonington or Newport; Sound Steamers to New York; Penna. R. R. to Philadelphia. *Rate,* $49.50.

Form X—198.—Choice of nine routes to Niagara Falls; thence via Toronto, Kingston, and Montreal to Quebec; thence to Alpine House (Gorham); stage to Glen House and North Conway; rail to Boston, and via Providence or Fall River to Stonington or Newport; Sound Steamers to New York; Penna. R. R. to Philadelphia. *Rate,* $49.25.

NIAGARA FALLS, N. Y., AND RETURN.—Continued.

Form X—200.—Choice of nine routes to Niagara Falls; thence via Lewiston, and Toronto to Montreal; thence via St. John's, West Farnham, Newport, and Wells River to Littleton; stage to Profile House and Bethlehem; rail to Fabyan and Crawford House and return to Fabyan; thence to Mt. Washington and Summit; stage to Glen House and North Conway; rail to Boston, and via Providence or Fall River to Stonington or Newport; Sound Steamers to New York; Penna R. R. to Philadelphia. *Rate*, $58.75.

Form X—202.—Choice of nine routes to Niagara Falls; thence via Lewiston, Toronto, Kingston, Prescott, Montreal, Sherbrooke, and Wells River to Littleton; stage to Profile House and Bethlehem; rail to Fabyan, Portland, Boston, and via Providence or Fall River to Stonington or Newport; Sound Steamers to New York; Penna. R. R. to Philadelphia. *Rate*, $50.25.

Form Ex. 1.—Choice of nine routes to Niagara Falls; thence via Lewiston, Toronto, Lake Ontario, or Grand Trunk R. R., Kingston, Thousand Islands, Alexandria Bay, Prescott, Rapids of the St. Lawrence River, Montreal, St. John's, St. Alban's, Highgate Springs, Burlington, Waterbury (Mansfield Mountain), Montpelier, White River Junction, Concord, Manchester, Nashua, and Lowell to Boston; Sound Steamers to New York; Penna. R. R. to Philadelphia. *Rate*, $38.75.

Form Ex. 2.—Choice of routes to Niagara Falls; thence via Lewiston, Toronto, Lake Ontario, or Grand Trunk R. R., Kingston, Ogdensburg, Thousand Islands, Alexandria Bay, Massena Springs, Alburgh Springs, St. Alban's, Burlington, Mansfield Mountain, White River Junction, Concord, and Nashua to Boston; Sound Steamers to New York; Penna. R. R to Philadelphia. *Rate*, $34.75.

Form Ex. 5.—Choice of nine routes to Niagara Falls; thence via Lewiston, Toronto, Lake Ontario, or Grand Trunk R. R., Kingston, Thousand Islands, Alexandria Bay, Ogdensburg, Alburgh Springs, St. Alban's, Burlington, Lake Champlain, Old Fort "Ti," Saratoga, and Albany to New York; Penna. R. R. to Philadelphia. *Rate*, $33.25.

Form Ex. 6.—Choice of nine routes to Niagara Falls; thence via Lewiston, Toronto, Kingston, Alexandria Bay, Thousand Islands, Ogdensburg, Alburgh Springs, St. Alban's, Burlington, Lake Champlain, Ticonderoga, Lake George, Caldwell, Glens Falls, Saratoga, Albany; Day Line Steamers to New York; Penna. R. R. to Philadelphia. *Rate*, $36.25.

Form Ex. 13.—Choice of nine routes to Niagara Falls; thence via Lewiston, Toronto, Kingston, Thousand Islands, Alexandria Bay, Ogdensburg, Alburgh Springs, St. Alban's (Mansfield Mountain), Montpelier, White River Junction, Bellows Falls, Springfield, Hartford, and New Haven to New York; Penna. R. R. to Philadelphia. *Rate*, $31.75.

Form Ex. 14.—Choice of nine routes to Niagara Falls; thence via Lewiston, Toronto, Kingston, Thousand Islands, Alexandria Bay, Prescott, Rapids of the St. Lawrence, Montreal, St. John's, Highgate Springs, St. Alban's, Burlington, Lake Champlain, Old Fort "Ti" to Saratoga; rail to Albany; Day or Night Boats to New York; Penna. R. R. to Philadelphia. (Via rail from Albany to New York, rate is 85 cents additional.) *Rate*, $36.70.

NIAGARA FALLS, N. Y., AND RETURN.—Continued.

Form Ex. 15.—Choice of nine routes to Niagara Falls; thence via Lewiston, Toronto, Kingston, Thousand Islands, Alexandria Bay, Prescott, Rapids of the St. Lawrence, Montreal, St. John's, Highgate Springs, St. Alban's, Burlington, Lake Champlain, Old Fort "Ti," Lake George, Caldwell, Glens Falls to Saratoga; rail to Albany; Day or Night Boats to New York; Penna. R. R. to Philadelphia. (Via rail from Albany to New York, rate is 85 cents additional.)
Rate, $39.45.

Form Ex. 16.—Choice of nine routes to Niagara Falls; thence via Lewiston, Toronto, Kingston. Thousand Islands, Alexandria Bay, Ogdensburg, Alburgh Springs, St. Alban's, Burlington, Lake Champlain, Old Fort "Ti" to Saratoga; rail to Albany; Day or Night Boats to New York; Penna. R. R. to Philadelphia. (Via rail from Albany to New York, rate is 85 cents additional.) *Rate,* $33.20.

Form Ex. 17.—Choice of nine routes to Niagara Falls; thence via Lewiston, Toronto, Kingston, Thousand Islands, Alexandria Bay, Ogdensburg. Alburgh Springs, St. Alban's, Burlington, Lake Champlain, Old Fort "Ti," Lake George, Caldwell, and Glens Falls to Saratoga; rail to Albany; Day or Night Boats to New York; Penna. R. R. to Philadelphia. (Via rail from Albany to New York, rate is 85 cents additional.) *Rate,* $36.20.

Form Ex. 20.—Choice of nine routes to Niagara Falls; thence via Lewiston, Toronto, Kingston, Thousand Islands, Alexandria Bay, Prescott, Rapids of the St. Lawrence, Montreal, St. John's. Highgate Springs, St. Alban's, Waterbury (Mansfield Mountain). Montpelier, White River Junction, Wells River, Littleton; stage to Profile House; stage to Bethlehem; rail to Twin Mountain House and Fabyan's; stage to Crawford House; rail to North Conway, Wolfboro, Lake Winnipesaukee, Weirs, Centre Harbor, Concord, Nashua, and Lowell to Boston; Sound Steamers to New York; Penna. R. R. to Philadelphia. *Rate,* $50.50.

Form Ex. 21.—Choice of nine routes to Niagara Falls; thence via Lewiston, Toronto, Kingston, Thousand Islands, Alexandria Bay, Ogdensburg, Alburgh Springs, St. Alban's, Burlington, Waterbury (Mansfield Mountain), Montpelier, White River Junction, Wells River, Littleton; stage to Profile House; stage to Bethlehem; rail to Twin Mountain House and Fabyan's; stage to Crawford House; rail to North Conway, Wolfboro, Centre Harbor, Lake Winnipesaukee, Weirs, Concord, Nashua, and Lowell to Boston; Sound Steamers to New York; Penna. R. R. to Philadelphia. *Rate,* $47.59.

Form Ex. 189.—Choice of nine routes to Niagara Falls; thence via Lewiston, Toronto, Kingston, Prescott, Rapids of the St. Lawrence, Montreal, St. John's, Highgate Springs, St. Alban's, Waterbury (Mansfield Mountain), Montpelier, Wells River, Littleton; stage to Profile House; stage to Bethlehem; rail to Twin Mountain House and Fabyan's; stage to Crawford House; rail to North Conway, Wolfboro, Lake Winnipesaukee, Centre Harbor, Weirs, Concord, and Nashua to Boston; Sound Steamers to New York; Penna. R. R. to Philadelphia.
Rate, $50.50.

Form Ex. 190.—Choice of nine routes to Niagara Falls; thence via Lewiston, Toronto, Kingston, Thousand Islands, Alexandria Bay, Ogdensburg, Alburgh Springs, St. Alban's, Waterbury (Mansfield Mountain), Montpelier, Wells River, Littleton; stage to Profile House; stage to Bethlehem; rail to Twin Mountain House and Fabyan's; stage to Crawford House; rail to North Conway, Wolfboro, Lake Winnipesaukee, Centre Harbor, Weirs, Concord, Nashua, and Lowell to Boston; Sound Steamers to New York; Penna. R. R. to Philadelphia.
Rate, $48.00.

NIAGARA FALLS, N. Y., AND RETURN.—Continued.

Form Ex. 193.—Choice of nine routes to Niagara Falls; thence via Lewiston, Toronto, Kingston, Thousand Islands, Alexandria Bay, Prescott, Rapids of the St. Lawrence, Montreal, St. John's, Highgate Springs, St. Alban's, Burlington, Waterbury (Mansfield Mountain), Montpelier, White River Junction, Wells River, Littleton; stage to Profile House; stage to Bethlehem; rail to Twin Mountain House and Fabyan's; stage to Crawford House; rail to North Conway; Eastern R. R. to Boston; Sound Steamers to New York; Penna. R. R. to Philadelphia.   *Rate,* $47.75.

Form Ex. 194.—Choice of nine routes to Niagara Falls; thence via Lewiston, Toronto, Kingston, Thousand Islands, Alexandria Bay, Ogdensburg, Alburgh Springs, St. Alban's, Burlington, Waterbury (Mansfield Mountain), Montpelier, White River Junction, Wells River, Littleton; stage to Profile House; stage to Bethlehem; rail to Twin Mountain House and Fabyan's; stage to Crawford House; rail to North Conway; Eastern R. R. to Boston; Sound Steamers to New York; Penna. R. R. to Philadelphia.   *Rate,* $45.25.

Form Ex. 195.—Choice of nine routes to Niagara Falls; thence via Lewiston, Toronto, Kingston, Thousand Islands, Alexandria Bay, Prescott, Rapids of the St. Lawrence, Montreal, St. John's, Highgate Springs, St. Alban's, Waterbury (Mansfield Mountain), Montpelier, Wells River, Littleton; thence via stage to Profile House; stage to Bethlehem; rail to Twin Mountain House and Fabyan's; stage to Crawford House; rail to North Conway; Eastern R. R. to Boston; Sound steamers to New York; Penna. R. R. to Philadelphia.   *Rate,* $47.75.

Form Ex. 206.—Choice of nine routes to Niagara Falls; thence via Lewiston, Toronto, Kingston, Thousand Islands, Alexandria Bay, Ogdensburg, Alburgh Springs, St. Alban's, Waterbury (Mansfield Mountain), Montpelier, Wells River, Littleton; stage to Profile House; stage to Bethlehem; rail to Twin Mountain House and Fabyan's; stage to Crawford House; rail to North Conway; Eastern R. R. to Boston; Sound Steamers to New York; Penna. R. R. to Philadelphia.   *Rate,* $45.25.

Form Ex. 276.—Choice of nine routes to Niagara Falls; thence via Lewiston, Toronto, Kingston, Thousand Islands, Alexandria Bay, Ogdensburg, Alburgh Springs, St. Alban's, Burlington, Lake Dunmore, Rutland, Bellows Falls, and Fitchburg to Boston; Sound Steamers to New York; Penna. R. R. to Philadelphia.   *Rate,* $34.75.

Form Ex. 279.—Choice of nine routes to Niagara Falls; thence via Lewiston, Toronto, Kingston, Thousand Islands, Alexandria Bay, Ogdensburg, Alburgh Springs, St. Alban's, Burlington, Waterbury (Mansfield Mountain), Montpelier, White River Junction, Wells River, Littleton, Twin Mountain House, Fabyan's, Bethelehem; stage to Profile House; stage to Plymouth; rail to Concord, Nashua, Lowell, and Boston; Sound Steamers to New York; Penna. R. R. to Philadelphia.   *Rate,* $47.50.

Form Ex. 285.—Choice of nine routes to Niagara Falls; thence via Lewiston, Toronto, Kingston, Prescott, Montreal, St. John's and Ticonderoga; stage to Roger's Rock Hotel; steamer to Caldwell; stage to Glens Falls; rail to Albany, and New York Central & Hudson River R. R. to New York; Penna. R. R. to Philadelphia.   *Rate,* $41.25.

Form Ex. 422.—Choice of nine routes to Niagara Falls; thence via Lewiston, Toronto, Kingston, Thousand Islands, Alexandria Bay, Prescott, Rapids of the St. Lawrence, Montreal, St. John's, Highgate Springs, St. Alban's, Burlington, Lake Dunmore, Rutland, Manchester, Lebanon Springs, Chatham 4 Corners, and N. Y. & Harlem R. R. to New York; Penna. R. R. to Philadelphia.   *Rate,* $37.50.

NIAGARA FALLS, N. Y., AND RETURN.—Continued.

Form Ex. 423.—Choice of nine routes to Niagara Falls; thence via Lewiston, Toronto, Kingston, Thousand Islands, Alexandria Bay, Ogdensburg, Alburgh Springs, St. Alban's, Burlington, Lake Dunmore, Rutland, Manchester, Lebanon Springs, Chatham 4 Corners, and N. Y. & Harlem R. R. to New York; Penna. R. R. to Philadelphia. *Rate,* $34.25.

Form Ex. 475.—Choice of nine routes to Niagara Falls; thence via Lewiston, Toronto, Kingston, Thousand Islands, Alexandria Bay, Prescott, Rapids of the St. Lawrence, Montreal, St. John's, Highgate Springs, St. Alban's, Burlington, Lake Dunmore, Rutland, Bennington, Manchester, State Line, Troy, and N. Y. Central & Hudson River R. R. to New York; Penna. R. R. to Philadelphia. *Rate,* $37.50.

RICHFIELD SPRINGS AND RETURN.

Form 15.—Philad'a & Reading R. R., via "Catawissa," to Williamsport. Northern Cent. R. W. to Elmira; Erie R. W. to Binghamton; Del., Lac. & West; R. R. to Richfield Springs; returning—Del., Lac. & West. R. R. to Scranton; Cent. R. R. of N. J. (L. & S. Div.) to Allentown; Allentown Street-Car Line to E. Penna. R. R. Junction (transfer included in ticket); Philad'a & Reading R. R. to Philadelphia. *Rate,* $16.55.

SARATOGA SPRINGS AND RETURN.

Form 16 (Via Troy).—Philad'a & Reading R. R., via "Catawissa," to Williamsport; Northern Cent. R. W. to Elmira; Erie R. W. to Binghamton; Delaware & Hudson Canal and R. R. to Albany; Delaware & Hudson Canal and R. R. to Saratoga Springs; returning—Delaware & Hudson Canal and R. R. to Albany; Hudson River Day or Night Boats to New York (transfer through New York not included); Cent. R. R. of N. J. to Easton; Leh. Val. R. R. to Allentown; Philad'a & Reading R. R. to Philadelphia. *Rate,* $18.20.

Form 17 (Via Troy).—Same as No. 16 to New York; thence via Penna. R. R. to Philadelphia. *Rate,* $17.50.

Form 69.—Philad'a & Reading R. R. to Allentown; Lehigh Valley R. R. to Waverly; Erie R.. W. to Elmira; Northern Central R. W. to Watkins'; Seneca Lake Nav. Co. to Geneva; New York Central & Hudson River R. R. to Schenectady; Delaware & Hudson Canal and R. R. to Saratoga Springs; returning—Delaware & Hudson Canal and R. R. to Albany; Hudson River Day Boats to New York (transfer through New York not included in ticket); Penna. R. R. to Philadelphia. *Rate,* $17.40.

WATKINS' GLEN AND RETURN.

Form 5.—Philad'a & Reading R. R., via "Catawissa," to Williamsport; Northern Cent. R. W. to Watkins'; returning—Northern Cent. R. W. to Williamsport; Penna. R. R. to Sunbury; Northern Cent. R. W. to Harrisburg; Philad'a & Reading R. R. to Philadelphia. *Rate,* $13.50.

Form 5—A.—Philad'a & Reading R. R., via "Catawissa," to Williamsport; Northern Cent. R. W. to Watkins'; returning same route. *Rate,* $12.00.

Form 6.—Philad'a & Reading R. R., via "Catawissa," to Williamsport; Northern Cent. R. W. to Watkins'; returning—Northern Cent. R. W. to Williamsport; Penna. R. R. to Sunbury; Northern Cent. R. W. to Harrisburg; Penna. R. R. to Philadelphia. *Rate,* $13.50.

WATKINS' GLEN AND RETURN.—Continued.

Form 7.—Philad'a & Reading R. R. to Harrisburg; Northern Cent. R. W. to Sunbury; Penna. R. R. to Williamsport; Northern Cent. R. W. to Watkins'; returning same route. *Rate*, $12.00.

Form 18 (Returning via Seneca and Cayuga Lakes).—Philad'a & Reading R. R., via "Catawissa," to Williamsport; Northern Cent. R. W. to Watkins' Glen; Seneca Lake Navigation Co. to Geneva; N. Y. Cent. & Hudson River R. R. to Cayuga; Wilcox Line of Steamers on Cayuga Lake to Ithaca; returning—Del., Lac. & West. R. R. to Owego; Erie R. W. to Binghamton; Del., Lac. & West. R. R. to Scranton; Cent. R. R. of N. J. (L. & S. Div.) to Allentown; Allentown Street-Car Line to E. Penna. R. R. Junction; Philad'a & Reading R. R. to Philadelphia. *Rate*, $14.85.

Form 23 (Returning via Saratoga).—Philad'a & Reading R. R., via "Catawissa," to Williamsport; Northern Cent. R. W. to Watkins; Seneca Lake Navigation Co. to Geneva; N. Y. Cent. & Hudson River R. R. to Schenectady; Del. & Hudson Canal and R. R. to Saratoga Springs, via Ballston Spa; returning—Del. & Hudson Canal and R. R. to Albany, via Troy; Hudson River Day or Night Boats to New York (transfer through New York not included in ticket); Penna. R. R. to Philadelphia. *Rate*, $17.65.

Form 27.—Philad'a & Reading R. R., via "Catawissa," to Williamsport; Northern Cent. R. W. to Watkins'; returning—Northern Cent. R. W. to Elmira; Erie R. W. to Waverly; Leh. Val. R. R. to Allentown; Philad'a & Reading R. R. to Philadelphia. *Rate*, $13.50.

Form 27—4.—Philad'a & Reading R. R. to Allentown; Leh. Val. R. R. to Elmira; Northern Cent. R. W. to Watkins'; returning—Northern Cent. R. W. to Williamsport; Philad'a & Reading R. R. to Philadelphia. *Rate*, $13.50.

Form 40 (Returning via New York).—Philad'a & Reading R. R. to Williamsport; Northern Cent. R. W. to Watkins'; returning—Northern Cent. R. W. to Elmira; Erie R. W. to New York; Penna. R. R. to Philadelphia. *Rate*, $16.60.

Form 58.—Philad'a & Reading R. R. to Allentown; Leh. Val. R. R. to Waverly; Erie R. W. to Elmira; Northern Cent. R. W. to Watkins'; returning same route. *Rate*, $12.00.

EXTENSION OR SIDE-TRIP TICKETS.

ALEXANDRIA BAY AND RETURN.

Form Ext. 3 (Thousand Islands).—Sold with any ticket to or passing Syracuse on N. Y. Cent. & Hudson River R. R.; Rome, Watertown & Ogdensburg R. R., Syracuse to Cape Vincent; Steamer "T. S. Faxton," Cape Vincent to Alexandria Bay and return to Cape Vincent; thence to Rome, via Rome, Watertown & Ogdensburg R. R. *Rate*, $7.00.

VIEW IN AU SABLE CHASM.

(57)

Form Ext. 5 (Thousand Islands).—Sold in connection with any ticket to or passing Utica, N. Y.; Utica & Black River R. R., Utica to Clayton; Steamer "J. H. Kelly," Clayton to Alexandria Bay; returning same route. *Rate*, $7.35.

Form Ex. 135.—Sold in connection with any ticket to or passing Ogdensburg; Ogdensburg to Alexandria Bay and return via steamer. *Rate*, $3.00.

AU SABLE CHASM AND RETURN.

Form X—96 (Fouquet's Hotel).—Sold in connection with any ticket to or passing Plattsburg. Via Lake Champlain Steamers to Port Kent, omnibus to Au Sable Chasm—coupon allowing holder free access to the Chasm; returning same route. *Rate*, $2.25.

Form Ex. 207.—Sold in connection with any ticket to or passing Burlington; via steamer to Port Kent; stage to Au Sable Chasm, and return same route. *Rate*, $1.75.

VIEW IN AU SABLE CHASM.

CACOUNA AND RETURN.

Form X—65.—Sold in connection with any ticket to or passing Quebec. Via Grand Trunk R. W., Royal Mail Line Steamers, or South Shore Express Line to Riviere Du Loup; thence by Intercolonial Railway to Cacouna; returning same route. *Rate, $4.50.*

CLAYTON AND RETURN.

Form Ext. 2 (Thousand Islands).—Sold with any ticket to or passing Syracuse on N. Y. Cent. & Hudson River R. R.; Rome, Watertown & Ogdensburg R. R., Syracuse to Cape Vincent; Steamer "T. S. Faxton" to Clayton; returning via same route to Sandy Creek Junction; thence to Rome, on N. Y. Cent. & Hudson River R. R. *Rate, $6.50.*

Form Ext. 4 (Thousand Islands).—Sold in connection with any ticket to or passing Utica, N. Y.; Utica & Black River R. R., Utica to Clayton; returning same route. *Rate, $6.50.*

GLEN ONOKO.

Form Ext. 1.—Sold in connection with any ticket to or passing Mauch Chunk. Mauch Chunk to Glen Onoko and return. *Rate, 25 cents.*

HA-HA BAY AND RETURN.

Form X—67.—Sold in connection with any ticket to or passing Quebec. Via Grand Trunk R. W., Royal Mail Line Steamers, or South Shore Express Line to Riviere du Loup; thence to Ha-Ha Bay; returning same route. *Rate, $8.50.*

Form Ex. 35.—Sold in connection with any ticket to or passing Quebec; Quebec to Ha-Ha Bay and return via steamer. *Rate, $9.00.*

LAKE GEORGE AND FORT TICONDEROGA.

Form X—14.—G (From Saratoga).—Sold in connection with any ticket to or passing Saratoga Springs. Delaware & Hudson Canal and R. R., Saratoga to Glen's Falls; thence to Caldwell via stage; thence to Baldwin via steamer on Lake George; thence to Saratoga via Delaware & Hudson Canal and R. R. *Rate, $6.90.*

Form X—14—B (From Saratoga).—Sold in connection with any ticket to or passing Saratoga Springs. Delaware & Hudson Canal and R. R., Saratoga to Baldwin; thence to Caldwell via Lake George Steamer; thence to Glen's Falls via stage; thence to Saratoga via Delaware & Hudson Canal and R. R. *Rate, $6.90.*

Form X—1—G (From Albany).—Sold in connection with any ticket to or passing Albany. Delaware & Hudson Canal and R. R., Albany to Glen's Falls; thence over same route as Form 14—G from Saratoga to Baldwin; thence to Albany via Delaware & Hudson Canal and R. R. *Rate, $9.35.*

Form X—1—B (From Albany).—Sold in connection with any ticket to or passing Albany. Delaware & Hudson Canal and R. R., Albany to Baldwin; thence over same route as per Form 14—W from Saratoga to Baldwin; thence to Albany via Delaware & Hudson Canal and R. R. *Rate*, $9.35.

MONTREAL AND RETURN.

Form Ex. 116.—Sold in connection with any ticket to or passing Burlington; Burlington via St. Alban's, Alburgh Springs, Ogdensburg, Rapids of the St. Lawrence to Montreal; returning via St. John's, Highgate Springs, and St. Alban's. *Rate*, $12.00.

VIEW IN AU SABLE CHASM.

OTTAWA CITY AND RETURN.

Form X—97.—Sold in connection with any ticket to or passing Prescott. Via St. Lawrence & Ottawa R. W.; returning same route. *Rate*, $4.00.

Form Ex. 109.—Sold in connection with any ticket to or passing Prescott; Prescott to Ottawa City and return via St. Lawrence and Ottawa R. R.
Rate, $4.00.

PAUL SMITH'S AND RETURN.

Form Ex. 80.—Sold in connection with any ticket to or passing Burlington; via steamer to Plattsburg; rail to Au Sable Station; stage to Paul Smith's, and return same route. *Rate*, $12.00.

Form Ex. 201.—Sold in connection with any ticket to or passing Malone; Malone to Paul Smith's and return (by stage). *Rate*, $8.00.

QUEBEC AND RETURN.

Form X—41.—Sold in connection with any ticket to or passing Montreal. Via Grand Trunk R. W., Royal Mail Line Steamers, or South Shore Express Line; returning same route. *Rate*, $5.00.

Form Ex. 18.—Sold in connection with any ticket to or passing Montreal; Montreal to Quebec and return via Grand Trunk R. R. or steamer. *Rate*, $5.00.

SACKETT'S HARBOR AND RETURN.

Form Ext. 7.—Sold in connection with any ticket to or passing Utica, N. Y.; Utica & Black River R. R., Utica to Sackett's Harbor; returning same route.
Rate, $5.00.

ST. ALBAN'S AND RETURN.

Form Ex. 79.—Sold in connection with any ticket to or passing Burlington; Burlington to St. Alban's via Central Vermont R. R. and return. *Rate*, $1.50.

STOWE AND RETURN.

Form Ex. 419.—Sold in connection with any ticket to or passing Waterbury; via stage to Stowe, and return same route. *Rate*, $2.00.

TADOUSAC AND RETURN.

Form X—66.—Sold in connection with any ticket to or passing Quebec. Via Grand Trunk R. W., Royal Mail Line Steamers, or South Shore Express Line to Riviere du Loup; thence to Tadousac; returning same route. *Rate*, $7.50.

TRENTON FALLS AND RETURN.

Form Ext. 6.—Sold in connection with any ticket to or passing Utica, N. Y.; Utica & Black River R. R., Utica to Trenton Falls; returning same route.

Rate, $1.25.

STEAM COLLIER.

SEA-SHORE EXCURSIONS.

ATLANTIC CITY AND RETURN.

Form 155 X.—Philad'a & Reading R. R. to Philadelphia; Camden & Atlantic R. R. (Vine street wharf) to Atlantic City; returning same route. (The tickets include transfer of baggage through Philadelphia each way, when checked from stations having through baggage checks.)

Phœnixville,	$4.15	Mahanoy City,	$6.85
Pottstown,	4.60	Shenandoah City,	7.30
Reading,	5.35	Shamokin,	7.90
Pottsville,	6.75	Danville,	8.70
Allentown,	5.75	Williamsport,	11.00
Harrisburg,	7.20	Norristown,	3.15
Tamaqua,	6.45		

BARNEGAT AND RETURN.

Form X—B.—Philad'a & Reading R. R. to Philadelphia; Penna. R. R. (Market street wharf) to Pemberton Junction; New Jersey Southern R. R. to Whiting's; Tuckerton R. R. to Barnegat; returning same route.

Reading,	$5.35	Harrisburg,	$7.21
Pottsville,	6.75		

BEACH HAVEN AND RETURN.
Tickets good until September 16th, 1876.

Form B. H.—Philad'a & Reading R. R. to Philadelphia; Penna. R. R. (Market street wharf) to Pemberton Junction; New Jersey Southern R. R. to Whiting's; Tuckerton R. R. to Beach Haven; returning same route.

Reading,	$6.35	Harrisburg,	$8.21
Pottsville,	7.75		

CAPE MAY AND RETURN.

Form 162 X.—Philad'a & Reading R. R. to Philadelphia; West Jersey R. R. (Market street wharf) to Cape May; returning same route. (Transfer of baggage included each way through Philadelphia, when checked from stations having through baggage checks.)

Phœnixville,	$5.15	Shenandoah City,	$8.80
Reading,	6.85	Shamokin,	9.40
Pottsville,	8.25	Danville,	10.20
Allentown,	7.25	Williamsport,	12.80
Harrisburg,	9.00	Norristown,	4.65
Tamaqua,	7.95		

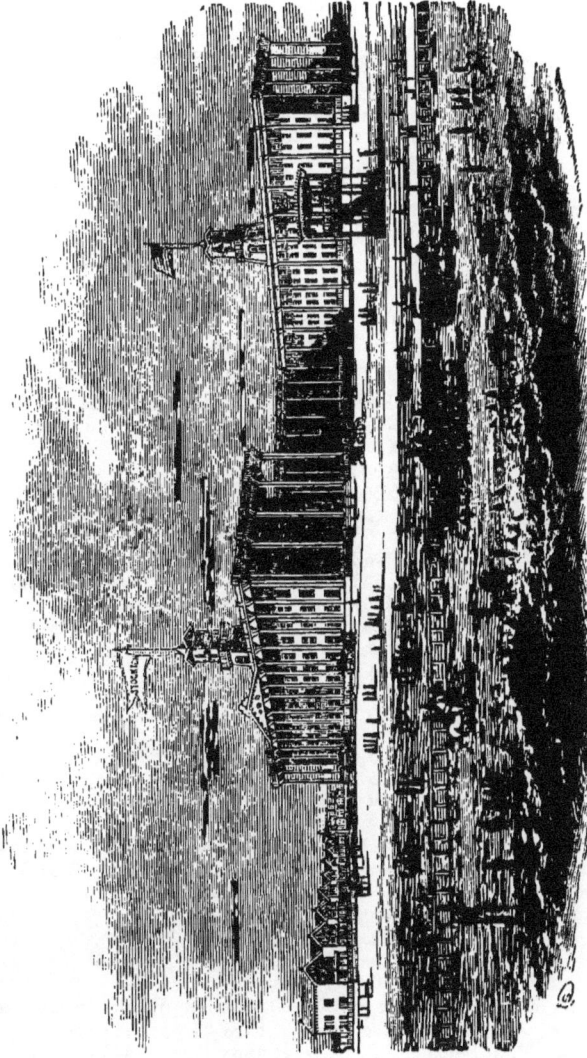

STOCKTON HOTEL, CAPE MAY, N. J.

APE MAY has an unrivaled surf and first-class hotel accommodations. Trains leave foot of Market street, Philadelphia, daily, Sundays excepted, at 9.00 A. M. and 3.15 P. M. Sundays at 7.30 A. M. Subject to change.

LONG BRANCH AND RETURN.

Form L. B. Exc.—Philad'a & Reading R. R. to Philadelphia; Penna. R. R. (West Philadelphia depot) to Monmouth Junction; Freehold & Jamesburg and N. J. Southern R. R. to Long Branch; returning same route.

Reading,	$6.35	Lebanon,	$7.45
Pottsville,	7.75	*Harrisburg,	8.70

*Includes transfer of baggage through Philadelphia, if checked with through check.

Form L. B. X. 2.—Philad'a & Reading R. R. to Philadelphia; Penna. R. R. (Market street wharf) to Pemberton Junction; N. J. Southern R. R. to Long Branch; returning same route.

Reading,	$6.35	*Harrisburg,	$8.70
Pottsville,	7.75	Rupert,	9.85
Lebanon,	7.45	*Williamsport,	12.50

*Includes transfer of baggage through Philadelphia, if checked with through check.

Form L. B. N. Y.—Philad'a & Reading R. R. to Tamanend; Leh. & Sus. and Cent. R. R. of N. J. to New York; Steamer to Sandy Hook; N. J. Southern R. R. to Long Branch; returning same route.

Rupert,	$9.25	Williamsport,	$12.00
Danville,	10.00		

NEW YORK AND LONG BRANCH.

Form S. S. X. 1.— Philad'a & Reading R. R. to Philadelphia; Penna. R. R. (Market street wharf) to Pemberton Junction; N. J. Southern R. R. to Long Branch (privilege of stopping off); thence to Sandy Hook and steamer "Plymouth Rock" to New York; returning—Cent. R. R. of N. J. (foot of Liberty street) to Easton; Leh. Val. R. R. to Allentown; Philad'a & Reading R. R. to destination.

Phœnixville,	$6.00	Catawissa,	$9.45
Reading,	6.00	Rupert,	9.55
Pottsville,	7.40	Danville,	9.85
Lebanon,	7.10	Milton,	10.45
Tamaqua,	7.60	Watsontown,	10.65
Lancaster,	7.65	Muncy,	11.10
Columbia,	7.80	*Williamsport,	12.00
*Harrisburg,	8.80		

*Includes transfer of baggage through Philadelphia, if checked with through check.

Form S. S. X. 3.—Same as Excursion S. S.—1 to New York; Cent. R. R. of N. J. to Tamanend; Philad'a & Reading R. R. to destination.

Catawissa,	$8.70	Watsontown,	$9.90
Rupert,	8.80	Muncy,	10.35
Danville,	9.10	*Williamsport,	11.35
Milton,	9.70		

*Includes transfer of baggage through Philadelphia, if checked with through check.

Form S. S. X. 4.—Philad'a & Reading R. R. to Tamanend; Cent. R. R. of N. J. to New York; N. J. Southern R. R., via Sandy Hook and Long Branch, to Pemberton Junction (privilege to stop off); Penna. R. R. to Philadelphia (Market street wharf); Philad'a & Reading R. R. to destination.

Catawissa,	$8.70	Watsontown,	$9.90
Rupert,	8.80	Muncy,	10.35
Danville,	9.10	*Williamsport,	11.35
Milton,	9.70		

*Includes transfer of baggage through Philadelphia, if checked with through check.

Form S. S. X. 5.—Philad'a & Reading R. R. to Allentown; Lehigh Valley R. R. to Easton; Central R. R. of New Jersey to Long Branch; returning same route.

Harrisburg, ... $9.55.

Form S. S. X. 6.—Philad'a & Reading R. R. to Tamanend; Central R. R. of New Jersey to Long Branch; returning same route.

Catawissa,	. . . . . . $8.40	Milton,	. . . . $9.40
Rupert,	. . . . 8.50	Muncy,	. . . . 10.05
Danville,	. . . . 8.80	Williamsport,	. . . . . . 10.75

LONG BRANCH AND NEWPORT.

Form S. S. X. 2.—Same as Excursion S. S.—1 to New York via Long Branch; thence via Old Colony Steamboat Co. ι, Newport or Fall River and return to New York; thence via Cent. R. R. of N. J. (foot of Liberty street) to Easton; Leh. Val. R. R. to Allentown; Philad'a & Reading R. R. to destination.

Phœnixville, .	. . . . . $13.00	Catawissa,	. . . . $16.45
Reading,	. . . . . . 13.00	Rupert,	. . . . 16.55
Pottsville,	. . . . . . 14.40	Danville,	. . . . 16.85
Lebanon,	. . . . . . 14.10	Milton,	. . . . 17.45
Tamaqua,	. . . . . . 14.60	Watsontown,	. . . . . . 17.65
Lancaster,	. . . . . . 14.65	Muncy,	. . . . 18.10
Columbia,	. . . . . . 14.80	*Williamsport,	. . . . . 19.00
*Harrisburg,	. . . . . 15.80		

*Includes transfer of baggage through Philadelphia, if checked with through check.

www.ingramcontent.com/pod-product-compliance
Lightning Source LLC
Chambersburg PA
CBHW021518090426
42739CB00007B/679

* 9 7 8 3 3 3 7 1 4 5 4 8 4 *